CW00515943

"We have loads of clients wh
Health and Safety. It's great
gives you enough informatio.. q-
Brilliant book."

**- Tony McKenna
Director of
Contractor Unlimited**

"Such a great book, very informative and helpful. It
made my mind up on how to tackle H&S with a
retained consultant."

**- Alan Dhillon
Director of
Probos Promotions Limited**

"Clear, concise information that does cut through
the red tape."

**- Mark Taylor
Director of
Lockfast Security Limited**

"Having worked alongside Ian and Neil and Acorn Safety Services for some time, their depth of knowledge and practical application is unparalleled"

- Stuart Williams
Managing Director of
Ace Car Care Ltd

"This was really helpful and made things so much clearer for our construction projects."

- Michael Bamling
Director of
Total Electrical Solutions

"This helps me when presenting project information to clients, they read this and just get it."

- Chris Penman
Director & Structural Engineer
STARK Consulting Engineers Ltd

Fear and Loathing of Health and Safety

Stay out of prison, avoid massive fines, and cut through the red tape

Ian Stone & Neil Munro

Don't Forget to Download
The #BONUS Materials for Free!

YOUR COMPANY LOGO

 ACORN SAFETY
SERVICES

Use the checklist on the next page to assess where you are at, what your business needs and how your progress is going. Make notes on any issues you face along the way and remember we're here to help you, if you need assistance just reach out to us:

www.acornhealthandsafety.co.uk / 01604 930 380

Item	Requirement
1. Health & Safety Policy	What is your policy on health and safety at work? You must include specific named people responsible, describe the practical arrangements you have in place to achieve the policy aims.
2. Risk Assessments Office	All work tasks need to be assessed - display screen assessments, desk assessments, slips, trips and falls etc.
3. Risk Assessments Site	All work tasks need to be assessed - use of tools, use of plant, traffic management etc
4. Risk Assessments Other Warehouse / Manufacturing Etc	All work tasks need to be assessed - forklifts, LEV's, use of machinery, manual handling
5. COSHH Assessments	What chemicals do you use? All must have an assessment from simple cleaning products through to more complex liquids or chemicals you use
6. Procedure Manual / Operating Procedure	How do you do things? Is there only one proper way to do things? How do you use that piece of equipment or machinery? It all needs to be documented.
7. Fire Risk Assessment	A fire risk assessment needs completing in and around your premises. Do you have everything in place? Signs, equipment escape routes etc
8. Trained Fire Marshall / Fire Wardens	Do you have the right amount of fire marshals and are they trained?
9. Asbestos Management Survey	All buildings older than 2000 may contain asbestos, a survey is the only way to be certain you know where it is.
10. Asbestos Register	Do you have a register of all the asbestos items on site?
11. Asbestos Management Plan	How are you managing your asbestos risk?
12. First Aid Kit	Do you have a proper kit in place?
13. First Aid Appointed Person	Have you appointed a responsible person?
14. Trained First Aider	Have you got appropriate trained staff in place?
15. Health and Safety Law Posters	Do you have the right posters displayed in the right location?
16. Consultation with Employees	Have you consulted with your employees regarding health and safety? Have you documented this?
17. Training Needs Analysis Completed	Have you carried out training needs analysis and recorded the results?
18. Training Completed	Have you completed the training identified from the training needs analysis?
19. Welfare Facilities Reviewed	Do you have the correct welfare provisions in place?
20. Provisions and Policy for Record Keeping	What are the provisions in place for policy and record keeping?
21. Competent Health and Safety Appointed Person	Who is your appointed competent health and safety person?

YOUR COMPANY NAME   HEALTH & SAFETY CHECKLIST   Page 1 of 2

Your Bonus Checklist!

All you have to do is go here:

www.acornhealthandsafety.co.uk/bonus

LEGAL NOTICES

Fear and Loathing of Health and Safety

Stay out of prison, avoid massive fines, and cut through the red tape

Ian Stone & Neil Munro

This book **cuts through Government regulation** red tape.

Find out the **easy way to select** a Health and Safety Consultant.

Discover how you can **avoid prison and massive fines**.

Table of Contents

INTRODUCTION   11

Why Bother?   **11**
Elf n Safety!   11

PREFACE   15

What can you expect?   **15**
What's in the book?   15

CHAPTER 1   17

What is Health and Safety?   **17**
What's it all really about?   17

CHAPTER 2   29

What's the Story?   **29**
A history lesson!   29

CHAPTER 3   79

Dreaded Government Regulations   **79**
The boring but needed bit   79

CHAPTER 4   85

Appointed Competent Health and Safety Person   **85**
Why most people need one   85

CHAPTER 5   95

Reasonably Practicable, Hazard and Risk   **95**
What do these terms actually mean?   95

CHAPTER 6   101

What do you need in place?   **101**
The core basics needed   101

Health & Safety Policies   **103**

Risk Assessments   **105**

COSHH Assessments   **115**

Procedure Manuals / Operating Procedures   **118**

Fire Risk Assessments   **128**

Fire Marshalls & Fire Wardens   **131**

Asbestos   **133**

First Aid   **143**

Health and Safety Law Posters   **147**

Consulting Employees   **149**

Training Needs   **152**

Welfare Facilities   **154**

Reporting Under RIDDOR   **156**

Keeping Records   **158**

Competent Person & Retained Consultants   **162**

CHAPTER 7   165

Additional Resources   **165**
    Additional information about health and safety   165

ABOUT THE AUTHORS   169

Ian Stone   **169**

ABOUT THE AUTHORS   173

Neil Munro   **173**

GLOSSARY   175

Glossary of Terms   **175**
    A list of the abbreviations and acronyms often used   175

Why Bother?

Elf n Safety!

Health and Safety is a very dry, arduous subject. Let us be totally honest right off the bat! Everyone has an opinion on it, and it's mostly bad.

The whole perceived premise around health and safety is that it's often "over the top", it's the "nanny state" handling, it's overbearing and "The Man" giving us extra things to do.

In reality it's there to keep us safe and healthy.

I'll admit it's often not done with the most gracious of methods and is often delivered in the most mind numbingly boring manner, which is why I think there is a great resistance to it.

It's also a great excuse that people use and band about for various reasons: "I can't mate, cos elf n safety said so."

The fact is, it is there to impose certain things on companies and individuals to ensure that we all go home the way we came into work.

Yes, it can be boring and yes it can be onerous, but it doesn't have to be that way. There is a new way to deal with the ever-increasing rules and regulations that are imposed on us all.

This book has been written from the two authors' perspectives with a view of cutting through all the complicated elements that surround health and safety and its management.

The chapters are packed to the brim with information and knowledge which will help you to understand and implement a good safety culture. This not only keeps you out of prison whilst avoiding massive fines but it also helps to keep people safe.

The book can be used as a reference guide to quickly help you bring your health and safety management in line.

For those that not only want to ensure compliance, but also want to educate themselves further, there's lots of information laced throughout this book.

If you're still unsure about any element of your health and safety management, there is a section at the back of the book whereby you can contact us for a zero cost zero commitment complimentary audit.

You now have everything in your power to step forward and proactively manage health and safety, but if you do want help in removing your headache, don't forget we're here to help you.

What can you expect?

What's in the book?

Bloody boring, nanny state, arse covering... these are some of the words that spring to most people's minds when it comes to health and safety.

On the whole it is boring, it's a boring subject that people don't quite get until the shit hits the fan. Then it's the most important thing they've ever wanted to understand.

When an accident happens at work it suddenly makes you sit up and think about it. Or if you don't care about the employees that work for you, I'll tell you what will grab your attention; sitting in front of a HSE officer being interviewed under caution (the same as police officers use). Trying to explain why you made the decisions to put or not put certain things in place, and why something major has happened, puts the fear into you because you don't know where this will all lead. You may even end up going to prison.

I understand the problem with it because it's boring AND complicated which makes for a double hit for most people to try and avoid.

Trying to decipher the reams and reams of regulations, approved codes of practice and guidance is a mammoth task for anyone.

Up until now, all you've really had to go on are the Health and Safety documents. They're really hard work for anyone... think of *War and Peace* but not as interesting a story to keep you motivated.

This is where we (Ian and Neil) have stepped in with this book. It simply cuts to the chase and avoids the bollox concerning all areas in and around health and safety.

We've worked together for over 18 years, being great friends, business partners and ultimately asbestos geeks. We joined forces to write this book to make your life easier.

Our observations come from working mainly in the asbestos field for nearly 20 years alongside many health and safety practitioners.

Behind us at Acorn Safety Services are a cracking team of health and safety experts that help clients every single day with the complicated workings of compliance.

They help clients stay on point and have also helped hone the book as you now see it. Essentially, this book is written from a toe in the water lay persons' perspective for lay people.

Wherever we can, we've simplified the overcomplicated information that surrounds health and safety, allowing you to be more informed to make the decisions you need, more quickly.

The book's main aim is to help people and businesses understand health and safety and to ultimately stop people being injured and even dying unnecessarily.

Remember though, you don't have to go it alone, we're only one step away www.acornhealthandsafety.co.uk

CHAPTER 1

What is Health and Safety?

What's it all really about?

Health and Safety has been around for millennia. It's what has kept us going as a race.

If we all acted like lemmings then we would have died out long, long ago.

Boiled right down at its core it's essentially what's behind the fight or flight mechanism that we as humans all have.

It's the telling your kids to be careful and to watch out for cars when crossing the road, it's why our ancestors quickly learned lessons of not eating certain foods, it's why some people are now (and rightly so) scared of spiders and snakes.

At its core, health and safety is about keeping us safe so that we can all go home the same way we went into work. It's about having the forethought to think about what needs to get done and the safest way possible to get it completed.

The problem with it however is that it has got a bad rep. It's often seen as draconian, nanny state or kid gloves, which I can certainly understand.

The press certainly don't help with making health and safety cool. They love nothing more than to print headlines and stories about businesses that can't operate because they've been shut down by elf n safety.

The thing about it all is that we as humans are still pretty stupid. There are dumbasses out there that try their damnedest to kill or injure themselves by doing bloody stupid things - it is beyond belief.

Take the TV show "You've Been Framed" for instance, each week there are hundreds of idiots doing really dumbass things which result in humorous injuries that we all love to watch.

There's also another show out there screening our amazing capabilities as a race which is "America's Dumbest Criminals", where each week they show some of the really stupid things that people do.

Another very dark humoured thing that is out there showcasing the human ability to do dumb things and die is "The Darwin Awards".

According to Wikipedia, "The awards are a tongue-in-cheek honour, originating in Usenet newsgroup discussions around 1985. They recognise individuals who have supposedly contributed to human evolution by selecting themselves out of the gene pool via death or sterility by their own actions.

The project became more formalised with the creation of a website in 1993 and was followed up by a series of books starting in 2000, authored by Wendy Northcutt. The criterion for the awards states, "In the spirit of Charles Darwin, the Darwin Awards commemorate individuals who protect our gene pool by making the ultimate sacrifice of their own lives. Darwin Award winners eliminate themselves in an extraordinarily idiotic manner, thereby improving our species' chances of long-term survival."

So, we know that we can do stupid things, right? We all do them; lose our keys, trip up, burn ourselves on the oven!

But that's where the split occurs between genuine everyday silly things that happen and the reason for taking health and safety as a business seriously.

I've said before that we all should go home in the manner we went into work, with all arms, legs, fingers and toes present. But the sad fact is that so many people don't and often it's not due to them being stupid or doing silly things, it's that an accident has happened that simply could have been avoided.

According to the HSE (Health and Safety Executive) there are some eye watering numbers of things going wrong.

Key figures for Great Britain (2018/19)

- 1.4 million working people suffering from a work-related illness *(That's more than the total population of Estonia)*

- 2,526 mesothelioma deaths due to past asbestos exposures (2017)

- 147 workers killed at work

- 581,000 working people sustaining an injury at work according to the Labour Force Survey *(That's more than the total population of Maldives)*

- 69,208 injuries to employees reported under RIDDOR

- 28.2 million working days lost due to work-related illness and workplace injury *(That's the equivalent of the entire population of Hong Kong [approx. 7.7m] being absent from work for an entire year!)*

- £15 billion estimated cost of injuries and ill health from current working conditions (2017/18) *(That's more than the Gross Domestic Product [GDP] of the country of Georgia)*

Crazy statistics right!? It's madness to think that in this day and age, 147 people died whilst at work in just one year. At work! They left their home in the morning and didn't return at the end of the day.

147
Fatal injuries to workers in 2018/19

Think about how many people have been affected, that 147 separate groups of families, friends, parents, and children are all now missing someone because something went horribly wrong whilst they were out working.

No one and I mean no one should die whilst out at work, there is simply no need. In this day and age, we have so many things that we can do and utilise to reduce the risks that we all face.

I know a lot of people that still think (wrongly) that health and safety is a burden and a massive cost. But when you compare it to the cost of things going wrong it's an insignificant sum to put in place. I'm not just talking about being hit in the pocket because of a big fine, I'm talking about the cost of injury or a life being taken. Can you imagine being someone's boss and having to make the call to someone's wife because a terrible accident has happened? It is a very sobering thought.

13,000 Deaths each year estimated to be linked to past exposure at work, primarily to chemicals or dust.

It's not just about deaths either, there are far too many serious injuries that occur each year.

498,000 Workers suffering from work-related musculoskeletal disorders (new or longstanding) in 2018/19

Manual handling, awkward or tiring positions and keyboard work or repetitive action are estimated to be the main causes of work-related musculoskeletal disorders based on 2009/10-2011/12 LFS data. That's right, something as simple as using a keyboard has contributed to 498,000 workers suffering from a musculoskeletal disorder.

Let's talk about the other costs for a minute. The hit you in the pocket kind of costs.

It's previously been reported that £1m fines are becoming more the norm in the UK for breaches to health and safety legislation.

The fact is that the HSE are becoming ever so more targeted with their approach and are less likely to give a bit of advice and let you be on your way. They target with precision and have been hitting with a 95% conviction rate.

So, if you get a visit from the HSE you damn well better be sure that your ducks are in a row!

Fee for Intervention Scheme

What is the fee for intervention scheme? In the words directly from the HSE *"If we visit your workplace and find that you are in material breach of health and safety law, you will have to pay for the time it takes us to identify what is wrong and to help you put things right. This is called a fee for intervention (FFI)."*

How much does it cost?

The HSE state:

"It currently costs £157 an hour. The fee will include the costs covering the time of the entire original visit. The total amount recovered will be based on the amount of time it takes HSE to identify the breach and help you put things right (including associated office work), multiplied by the hourly rate.

Your fee may include the inspector's time:

- *at your business or workplace*
- *preparing reports*
- *getting specialist advice*
- *talking to you after the visit*
- *talking to your workers*

The fee can vary depending on:

- *how long the original visit was*
- *the time the inspector spent helping you put things right*
- *the time it took the inspector to investigate your case*
- *any time we spend on taking action against you"*

Yes, that's an eye watering £157.00 or one hundred and fifty seven pounds per hour! You have to essentially pay for the privilege of HSE putting their case together against you which may end up going to court where you then face their conviction hit rate of 95% which can lead to possible custodial sentences, fines and court costs!

Also, as the icing on the cake, the HSE invoice terms state that you must pay any invoice they send within 30 days, too.

Did we forget to mention Prison?

So, on top of all that money you also run the risk of ending up in one of Her Majesty's pleasure facilities. A quick google reveals lots of cases whereby people are sent to prison, and this covers both company directors and company employees to boot.

If you've done wrong and are found out it can certainly cost you a lot of money and time. The figures reveal that prosecution rates are on the up, fines are on the up, and prison sentences are on the up, so overall for those looking to flout the law it's not looking good.

So now hopefully you can see that the concept behind health and safety is to keep us safe. There is a huge range in injuries that can occur, and we need to stop this from happening.

But thankfully, you're one of the good guys, which is why you're reading this book! So well done to you, by reading this you're already doing 90% more than those out there and starting to protect yourself right now.

We know that by not complying with health and safety rules and regulations you run the risk of building up some pretty big costs pretty quickly which is why we urge you to get ahead of the game.

So, to avoid this happening to you, in the next few chapters we will be covering the history of health and safety and what is needed to be done so you don't fall foul.

CHAPTER 2

What's the Story?

A history lesson!

Health and safety as we now know it isn't a new thing - it's not modern by any means. It will probably surprise you that it dates back to 1833!

The Health and Safety Executive have a long history here in the UK. Below is the HSE's own history as described by them:

1833 HM Factory Inspectorate was formed

The first factory inspectors were appointed under the provisions of the Factories Act 1833. Initially their main duty was to prevent injury and overworking in child textile workers. The four inspectors were responsible for approximately 3,000 textile mills and had powers to enter mills and question workers. They were also able to formulate new regulations and laws to ensure the Factories Act could be suitably enforced. Despite serious opposition from contemporary politicians and employers, the factory inspectors were enthusiastic and were able to influence subsequent legislation relating to machinery guarding and accident reporting. By 1868 there were 35 inspectors and sub-inspectors, each responsible for a distinct geographical area. Changes to legislation during the period 1860 to 1871 extended the Factories Act to practically all workplaces and the inspectors took on the role of technical advisers in addition to their enforcement duties. Major technological developments, world wars and the changing nature of employment have provided a constant challenge to factory inspectors over subsequent years.

1843 Mines Inspectorate was formed

In 1840 a Royal Commission was established to investigate working conditions in the mining industry. The Commission's findings published in 1842 made shocking reading. Accidents, brutality, lung diseases, long hours and highly dangerous and adverse working conditions were found to be the norm. Public outcry resulted and the Mines Act 1842 was brought into force.

The Act allowed for the appointment of an inspector of mines and collieries and the first inspector, Hugh Seymour Tremenheere, took up his post in 1843. Tremenheere had only limited powers under the Act but undertook many prosecutions, investigated the condition of the mining community and made recommendations for training managers, reporting of fatal and serious accidents and provision of pithead baths and suitable habitation for mine workers. In 1850 inspectors were allowed to enter and inspect mine premises and Tremenheere's plans for a dedicated mining inspectorate began to be realised.

1893 The first women factory inspectors were appointed

The Factory Inspectorate was formed in 1833 and for the first 60 years it employed only male inspectors. Alexander Redgrave, the Chief Inspector of Factories, was opposed to the idea of women inspectors, saying in his 1879 annual report:

"I doubt very much whether the office of factory inspectors is one suitable for women... The general and multifarious duties of an inspector of factories would really be incompatible with the gentle and home-loving character of a woman..."

After several years of campaigning by the Women's Protective and Provident League, the London Women's Trades Council and others, amid growing support in Parliament, the first "Lady Inspectors", May Abraham and Mary Paterson, were appointed in 1893. They were based in London and Glasgow respectively and earned an annual salary of £200. Much of their early work involved enforcing the Truck Acts, investigating women's hours of employment and enforcing health and safety in laundries.

1895 The Quarry Inspectorate was formed

Prior to the Quarries Act 1894, the only quarries that factory inspectors were responsible for inspecting were quarries using steam power. The introduction of the Quarries Act 1894 extended the powers of the Metalliferous Mines Regulation Act 1872 to give inspectors the power to enforce provisions of notifying accidents, undertake prosecutions and make Special Rules. This led to the establishment of the Quarry Inspectorate.

1956 Agriculture (Safety, Health and Welfare Provisions) Act

This Act introduced comprehensive health protection and safeguards for agricultural workers and for children who may come into contact with agricultural machinery, equipment or vehicles. It prohibited the lifting of excessive weights, outlined the general provisions that must be made for sanitary conveniences and washing facilities and stipulated requirements for first aid provision. The Act also laid down requirements for the notification and investigation of accidents and diseases. It was instrumental in appointing a number of inspectors with the powers to enter agricultural premises and enforce the Act.

1959 Nuclear Installations Act 1959 which established the Nuclear Installations Inspectorate

The investigation into a major incident at the Windscale nuclear site on 8 October 1957 led to a recommendation from the United Kingdom Atomic Energy Authority (UKAEA) that a body should be set up with responsibility for licensing future civil reactors in the UK. The insurance industry added pressure to the debate and in 1959 the Nuclear Installations Act was passed, setting in train the formation of the Inspectorate of Nuclear Installations within the Ministry of Power. Today's Nuclear Installations Inspectorate (NII) is responsible for the UK safety regulation of nuclear power stations, nuclear chemical plants, defence nuclear facilities, nuclear safety research, decommissioning and strategy. Since 2 April 2007 NII has also been responsible for civil nuclear operational security and safeguards matters.

1974 Flixborough chemical plant explosion (28 fatalities)

On Saturday 1 June 1974 a massive explosion destroyed a large part of the Nypro (UK) Ltd plant at Flixborough, near Scunthorpe. Twenty-eight people were killed in the incident and thirty-six people suffered injuries. More casualties could have been expected if the incident had occurred on a weekday. Widespread damage was caused to surrounding commercial premises and residential housing. The explosion resulted from the ignition and deflagration of a huge vapour cloud which formed when cyclohexane under pressure escaped from a part of the plant used in the production of cyclohexanone and cyclohexanol. Her Majesty's Factory Inspectorate investigated the incident (this was before the Health and Safety Executive was formed) and produced an interim report. Following on from this, a formal investigation into the circumstances surrounding the explosion was undertaken by a Court of Inquiry chaired by Roger J. Parker QC.

"a bold and far-reaching piece of legislation"

The Health and Safety at Work etc Act 1974 was described as "a bold and far-reaching piece of legislation" by HSE's first Director General, John Locke. It certainly marked a departure from the framework of prescribed and detailed regulations which was in place at the time. The Act introduced a new system based on less-prescriptive and more goal-based regulations, supported by guidance and codes of practice. For the first time, employers and employees were to be consulted and engaged in the process of designing a modern health and safety system. The Health and Safety at Work etc Act 1974 also established the Health and Safety Commission (HSC) for the purpose of proposing new regulations, providing information and advice and conducting research. HSC's operating arm, the Health and Safety Executive was formed shortly after in order to enforce health and safety law, a duty shared with Local Authorities.

Health and Safety Commission established

The Health and Safety Commission (HSC) was formed when the Health and Safety at Work etc Act 1974 received Royal Assent on 31 July 1974. HSC's constitution and responsibilities were laid out in Sections 1, 10 and 11 of the Act and, according to the first HSC annual report (1977) included: "taking appropriate steps to secure the health, safety and welfare of people at work, to protect the public generally against risks to health and safety arising out of the work situation, to give general direction to the Health and Safety Executive (HSE) and guidance to Local Authorities on the enforcement provisions of the Act, to assist and encourage persons with duties under the Act and to make suitable arrangements for research and the provision of information." Some of the key health and safety hazards which HSC was concerned with in its first few months included asbestos, construction, dusts, genetic manipulation, ionising radiation, lead, noise and vinyl chloride.

1975 Health and Safety Executive was formed

The Health and Safety Executive (HSE) was formed on 1 January 1975 under the leadership of its first Director, John Locke. HSE's remit was to undertake the requirements of the Health and Safety Commission and to enforce health and safety legislation in all workplaces, except those regulated by Local Authorities. A number of regulatory and scientific organisations transferred to HSE at this time, including: the Factory Inspectorate; Explosives Inspectorate; Employment Medical Advisory Service; Nuclear Installations Inspectorate; Safety and Health Division from the Department of Energy; the Mines Inspectorate; the Safety in Mines Research Establishment; the British Approvals Service for Electrical Equipment in Flammable Atmospheres; and the Alkali and Clean Air Inspectorate. One of the first tasks undertaken by HSE was the re-organisation of the Factory Inspectorate into a series of 21 Area Offices and 11 local offices, supported by Field Consultant Groups, comprised of specialist scientific and technical staff.

First HSC advisory committees established

The Health and Safety Commission (HSC) set up the first of a number of advisory committees during 1975. This was done with a view to drawing upon the expertise of industry and specialist organisations and in encouraging wide participation in the improvement of occupational health and safety. Advisory committees on the following topics were set up over the next couple of years: Advisory Committee on Dangerous Substances; Advisory Committee on Toxic Substances; Medical Advisory Committee; Advisory Committee on Asbestos; Advisory Committee on Major Hazards; Advisory Committee on the Safety of Nuclear Installations; Safety in Mines Research Advisory Board; and the British Approvals Service for Electrical Equipment In Flammable Atmospheres (BASEEFA) Advisory Council. HSC also consulted the Trades Union Congress (TUC) and Confederation of British Industry (CBI) for suggestions for additional advisory bodies. A full list of contemporary advisory committees is available.

1976 First HSC annual report published

The first annual report published by the Health and Safety Commission (HSC) concentrated on three strategic aims, namely: encouraging positive attitudes to health and safety in the workplace; developing better information about the cause and scale of hazards; and the review of section 1(2) of the Health and Safety at Work etc Act 1974. The report also outlined the objectives of the Health and Safety Executive (HSE) and Health and Safety Commission (HSC), the scope of the Health and Safety at Work etc Act 1974 and policy development.

1977 Safety Representatives and Safety Committees Regulations 1977 (S.I. 1977/500)

These regulations established the right of a recognised trade union to appoint safety representatives from among the employees it represented. The exception to this was employees of mines, specifically coal mines as defined by section 180 of the Mines and Quarries Act 1954. The regulations conferred a number of powers to safety representatives including: "to investigate potential hazards and dangerous occurrences at the workplace (whether or not they are drawn to his attention by the employees he represents) and to examine the causes of accidents at the workplace"; "to make representations to the employer on general matters affecting the health, safety or welfare of the employees at the workplace"; and to inspect certain documents. Under the terms of the regulations, two or more safety representatives could request their employer to establish a safety committee. The regulations also outlined the terms for pay for time off allowed to safety representatives carrying out official duties.

1979 Golborne Colliery disaster (10 fatalities)

Ten people died and one person was seriously injured when firedamp ignited and exploded in the Plodder Seam at the Golborne Colliery in the Greater Manchester area on 18 March 1979. Firedamp accumulated following a breakdown in the ventilation system and it is thought that this was probably ignited by electrical sparking. The Health and Safety Executive's Safety in Mines Research Establishment (SMRE) investigated the incident and made recommendations for improving both ventilation systems and intrinsically safe electrical equipment in mines.

1980 Control of Lead at Work Regulations 1980 (S.I. 1980/1248)

The Regulations stipulated that where employees are exposed to lead in the workplace, employers or those who are self-employed must assess the work in order to establish the nature and degree of the exposure to lead. Employers are also required to provide information, training and instruction to exposed workers. Other requirements under the Regulations included: ensuring control measures are in place for material, plant and processes and that these are properly maintained; providing washing and changing facilities and areas for employees to eat, drink and smoke; avoiding the spread of contamination; cleaning; air monitoring; and conducting medical surveillance and biological tests.

Notification of Accidents and Dangerous Occurrences Regulations 1980 (S.I. 1980/637)

The Notification of Accidents and Dangerous Occurrences Regulations 1980 (NADOR) required employers and the self-employed to keep a record of any accidents or certain types of dangerous occurrences and report these to HSE. The Regulations include lists of the types of dangerous occurrences that are reportable, including those that occur in any situation and those that relate specifically to mines, quarries and railways. Today, the Reporting of Injuries, Diseases and Dangerous Occurrences Regulation 1995 (RIDDOR) has replaced NADOR.

1981 Health and Safety (First Aid) Regulations 1981 (S.I. 1981/917)

These Regulations which came into force on 1st July 1982 stipulated that "an employer shall provide or ensure that there are provided, such equipment and facilities as are adequate and appropriate in the circumstances for enabling first aid to be rendered to his employees if they are injured or become ill at work." Employers were also required to inform employees about the arrangements in place for providing first-aid, including the location of facilities, personnel and equipment. Self-employed people were also covered by the Regulations as there was a requirement for them to provide appropriate and adequate equipment for rendering first aid to themselves at work, if necessary.

1983 150th anniversary of HM Factory Inspectorate

Today, HSE's factory inspectors are based in the Field Operations Directorate.

HSE starts to enforce asbestos licensing industry

The Health and Safety Commission's Advisory Committee on Asbestos reached agreement on two European Union directives concerning the protection of workers exposed to asbestos and the marketing and use of asbestos. This agreement, based on medical evidence and research on engineering controls resulted in the development of the Asbestos (Licensing) Regulations 1983 which came into force on 1 August 1984.

Asbestos (Licensing) Regulations 1983 (S.I. 1983/1649)

The Asbestos (Licensing) Regulations 1983 came into force on 1 August and have been amended by several pieces of legislation in the intervening years. At the time the Regulations became law, no-one could carry out work with asbestos insulation including asbestos insulation board or asbestos coating unless they held a licence granted by HSE or worked for someone who held such a licence. There were three exemptions to the requirements, namely: collecting samples or air monitoring to identify asbestos; work carried out with asbestos insulation, asbestos insulating board or asbestos coating by employers or the self-employed, either by themselves or by using their own employees and in their own premises; and work of short duration using these materials.

HSE starts to enforce genetic manipulation regulations

HSE assumed responsibility for enforcing the Health and Safety (Genetic Manipulation) Regulations 1978 from the Department of Education and Science in 1983. In March 1984 a new Advisory Committee on Genetic Manipulation (ACGM) was set up to support this new role. In its first year, ACGM set up working parties to investigate: the release of genetically manipulated organisms for agricultural and environmental purposes; the uses of viruses in genetic manipulation, including the use of recombinants containing potentially harmful nucleic acid sequences; and monitoring of workers involved in genetic manipulation work. In 2004, ACGM was replaced by the Scientific Advisory Committee on Genetic Modification (Contained Use), (SACGM(CU)). SACGM(CU) provides technical and scientific advice to the UK Competent Authority on all aspects of the human and environmental risks of the contained use of genetically modified organisms.

1984 HSE starts to enforce domestic gas safety

HSE assumed responsibility for mains gas safety functions on 1 February 1984, taking over from the Department of Energy. This involves responsibility for the safety of gas mains in the home as well as the workplace. HSE was given the power to introduce gas safety regulations under the Gas Act 1972 and enforce safety regulations made under this Act. Now HSE and local authorities have joint enforcement responsibilities under the Gas Safety (Installation and Use) Regulations 1998 and are responsible for preventing injury to consumers and the public from either fire and explosion or carbon monoxide (CO) poisoning.

Abbeystead pumping station (16 fatalities)

An explosion occurred at a subterranean valve house in the Lune/Wyre Water Transfer Scheme at Abbeystead in Lancashire on 23 May 1984. Sixteen people were killed and 28 injured whilst taking part in an evening visit at the site. The visit was part of a programme to demonstrate to local residents that their fears that the Transfer Scheme would cause winter flooding were unfounded. The explosion occurred while water was being pumped over the weir into the river Wyre. The valve house was severely damaged during the incident. HSE investigated and concluded that the explosion was caused by the ignition of a mixture of methane and air which had built up in the wet room of Abbeystead Valve House. The source of the ignition was not identified. HSE also contacted water authorities and alerted them to the potential dangers of water transfer and comparable systems where methane could pose a serious risk.

Control of Industrial Major Accident Hazard Regulations 1984 (S.I. 1984/1902)

The Regulations, known as CIMAH, require that safe operation can be demonstrated for industrial activities in which various substances as defined in Schedule I of the Regulations are involved. They also set out requirements for isolated storage of substances in Schedule 2 of the Regulations. Under the Regulations, manufacturers are required to provide written evidence that major accident hazards have been identified and the necessary steps put in place to prevent major incidents and protect workers on the site. They are also required to prepare an off-site emergency plan to complement the Local Authority emergency plan and to provide information to the Local Authority which can be used to inform people living in the locality who might be affected by a CIMAH site.

1985 Reporting of Injuries, Diseases and Dangerous Occurrences Regulations 1985 (S.I. 1985/2023)

The Reporting of Injuries, Diseases and Dangerous Occurrences Regulations 1985, commonly known as 'RIDDOR', require a 'responsible person' to notify the enforcing authority where a person dies or sustains any injuries or specific medical conditions or where a dangerous occurrence takes place in connection with a work activity. The Regulations set out the specific injuries which are reportable including fractures, amputation, decompression sickness and others. A list of the dangerous occurrences reportable under RIDDOR is provided in Schedule 1 of the Regulations, while a second schedule sets out reportable diseases under RIDDOR. Separate notification requirements for mines, quarries and railways are also explained.

Putney domestic gas explosion (8 fatalities)

Eight residents were killed in a major explosion which occurred on 10 January 1985 at a block of luxury flats in Newnham House, Manor Fields, Putney, South London. HSE worked with investigation teams from the British Gas Corporation, South Eastern Gas, Midland Research Station, the London Borough of Wandsworth and the police and fire authority to ascertain the cause of the incident. Investigations revealed the explosion was caused by gas leaking into the building from a crack in the cast iron pipe that formed the gas main. The crack had been caused by uneven loading on the pipe due to differential settlement. HSE made a number of recommendations regarding the safety of gas mains, one of the key ones being for the British Gas Corporation to review its priorities for replacing cast iron gas mains.

HSE starts to enforce transport of dangerous goods by road safety

Legislation surrounding the regulation of dangerous goods has been subject to many changes since HSE began enforcing The Dangerous Substances (Conveyance by Road in Packages) Regulations 1986 (PGR). Today, HSE is one of the organisations responsible for enforcing The Carriage of Dangerous Goods and Use of Transportable Pressure Receptacles Regulations 2009 (CDG 2009).

Fire at Bradford City Football Stadium - Valley Parade

Fifty-six people died and approximately 256 were injured when a serious fire broke out in the main stand at Valley Parade, the home ground of Bradford City Football Club, on Saturday 11 May 1985. HSE investigated this incident, described as the worst fire disaster in the history of British football. Forensic tests concluded that the fire was probably started by a dropped match or a cigarette stubbed out in a polystyrene cup. The old wooden stands that had been in place for decades at the ground contributed to the ferocity of the fire. The disaster prompted a review of the UK's sports grounds and stadia, resulting in legislative changes.

Ionising Radiations Regulations 1985 (1985 No 1333)

The Ionising Radiations Regulations 1985 applied to any work with ionising radiation except work carried out under section 1 of the Nuclear Installations Act 1965 and in certain activities as outlined in Schedule 3 of the Regulations. The Regulations set out legal duties in the following areas: dose limitation including restriction of exposure; designation of controlled areas and of classified persons; appointment of qualified persons; training and instruction requirements; dosimetry and medical surveillance; control of radioactive substances including arrangements for personal protective equipment and washing and changing facilities; assessment of hazards; investigation of cases of overexposure; and fees for medical examinations.

1986 HSE starts to enforce pesticide safety

The Control of Pesticides Regulations 1986 (S.I. 1986/1510) conferred authority on HSE to enforce pesticide safety. The Regulations provided a detailed list of those types of pesticides which are subject to control and those which are excluded. They also outlined the approvals required before any pesticides could be sold, stored, used, supplied or advertised. In addition, the Regulations set out the general conditions for pesticides regarding sale, supply, storage, advertisement and use, including aerial application. The Regulations were superseded by the Control of Pesticides Regulations 1997 (S.I. 1997/188).

1987 Control of Asbestos at Work Regulations 1987 (S.I. 1987/2115)

These regulations stipulate that an employer 'shall not carry out any work which exposes or is liable to expose any of his employees to asbestos unless either a) before commencing that work he has identified, by analysis or otherwise, the type of asbestos involved in the work; or b) he has assumed that the asbestos is crocidolite or amosite and for the purposes of the Regulations has treated it accordingly'. Under the Regulations, employers must notify the enforcing authority of work with asbestos in certain circumstances. They must also provide information, instruction and training for employees who are liable to be exposed to asbestos during the course of their work. Adequate control measures must be in place and must be adequately maintained to prevent or reduce the spread of asbestos. Other requirements of the regulations include: ensuring cleanliness of plant and premises; designation of areas where asbestos is present; air monitoring including associated record-keeping; medical surveillance and keeping health records; provision of washing and changing facilities; and storage and labelling of raw asbestos and asbestos waste.

King's Cross underground station fire (31 fatalities)

The King's Cross underground station fire occurred on 18 November 1987. Thirty-one people died and many more were injured. The fire started when a lighted match which was dropped by a passenger on one of the station's escalators fell through a gap between the treads and skirting boards and set fire to grease and dust that had been allowed to accumulate. The resulting fire spread rapidly, accompanied by thick black smoke. As London Underground's practice was to call the Fire Brigade only when a fire seemed to be getting out of hand, by the time the Fire Brigade arrived, the fire was widespread and out of control. There were no smoke detectors in place in the station and only a manual water spray system. The Fennell Inquiry report noted that the London Underground staff members on duty were poorly trained and "woefully unequipped to meet the emergency that arose". Following the incident, London Underground and the other organisations involved in the incident accepted 157 recommendations for safety improvements outlined in the official report.

1988 Control of Substances Hazardous to Health Regulations (S.I. 1988/1657)

The Control of Substances Hazardous to Health Regulations, generally referred to as the COSHH Regulations, were introduced to protect the health of people arising from work activities. Under the Regulations, employers must carry out a risk assessment to ensure that employees are not exposed to substances which will be hazardous to their health. Where exposure to such substances cannot be prevented, employers must provide suitable protective equipment and control measures and they must ensure that such equipment is adequately maintained, examined and tested and the results of tests recorded and kept. RIDDOR stipulates a requirement for monitoring exposure in the workplace and maintaining suitable records. It also sets out requirements for health surveillance and medical surveillance. Employers are also obliged to ensure that where exposure to hazardous substance is unavoidable, workers are made aware of the associated health risks and the precautions that should be taken including any associated instruction and training requirements.

Clapham train crash (35 fatalities)

A major rail accident occurred on the morning of 12 December 1988 at Clapham Junction when two commuter trains collided and were subsequently hit by a third empty train. Thirty-five people died in the accident and many other passengers sustained injuries. The Inquiry into the collision concluded that the main cause was 'wiring issues' and it laid the blame on British Rail work practices. The Inquiry also made 93 recommendations for safety improvements to be made. These included a limit to the hours that signalmen should be allowed to work and a system of automatic train protection (ATP) to be installed.

Piper Alpha oil installation fire and explosion (167 fatalities)

A series of catastrophic explosions occurred on the Piper Alpha offshore platform on the evening of 6 July 1988. This led to a major and sustained gas fire which resulted when the Tartan gas riser ruptured. The majority of the emergency systems including the fire water system failed to operate and the resulting fierce fires and dense smoke made evacuation by helicopter or lifeboats impossible. Structural collapse of the platform quickly followed, causing many of the offshore workers to jump into the sea. Of the 226 people on board the Piper Alpha platform, 165 died and two members of the 'Sandhaven's' fire rescue craft lost their lives. The Lord Cullen inquiry into the incident made a series of recommendations for the future regulation of the offshore installations and appointed the Health and Safety Executive as a single regulatory body to enforce occupational health and safety in the offshore oil and gas industry.

1989 Noise at Work Regulations 1989 (S.I. 1989/1790)

The Noise at Work Regulations 1989 stipulate that 'Every employer shall reduce the risk of damage to the hearing of his employees from exposure to noise to the lowest level reasonably practicable'. To this end, the Regulations require that a noise assessment should be made if employees are likely to be exposed to the first action level or above or to the peak action level of noise. The assessment should be reviewed as appropriate and adequate assessment records kept.

Where employees are exposed to noise, adequate ear protection must be provided and ear protection zones set up where necessary. Any equipment provided must be carefully maintained and used and employees should be given information on the steps they can take to protect their hearing in the workplace. The Regulations also outline the particular modifications of the duties of manufacturers of articles for use at work and articles of fairground equipment in relation to the Regulations.

Electricity at Work Regulations 1989 (S.I. 1989/635)

The Electricity at Work Regulations 1989 had a wide remit, covering: work systems, protective equipment and work activities; adverse or hazardous environments; capability and strength of electrical equipment; earthing and other suitable precautions; electrical protection, insulation and placing of conductors; connections; integrity of conductors; cutting off electrical supply and isolation; working on dead equipment; working on or in the vicinity of live conductors; working space, lighting and access; and competent persons. A section of the Regulations applied only to Mines, covering areas such as: introduction of electrical equipment; restrictions in certain underground zones; provisions associated with the presence of firedamp; approval of certain equipment in safety-lamp mines; cutting off electricity to circuits underground; oil-filled equipment; electric shock notices; information and records; use of battery-powered locomotives and vehicles into safety-lamp mines; and storage, transfer and charging of electrical storage batteries.

Hillsborough disaster

The Hillsborough Stadium disaster in which 96 people were killed and 170 injured was one of Britain's worst sporting disasters. The disaster occurred on 15 April 1989 at the Hillsborough football stadium during the FA Cup semi-final match between Nottingham Forest and Liverpool. Football fans were caught up in a massive crush which occurred as a result of too many Liverpool fans being let into a full stand at the Leppings Lane end of the stadium. The resulting surge of fans gaining access to the ground caused the fans already inside the ground to be pushed against the wire safety fences and crushed. Lord Justice Taylor's official inquiry into the disaster led to many new safety measures being introduced to sporting stadia.

1990 HSE starts to enforce rail safety

Responsibility for railway safety passed from the Department of Transport to HSE in 1990. This took place because the Department of Transport's Railway Inspectorate was heavily criticised for their poor protection of rail passengers and for not employing modern risk assessment techniques. The transfer was also seen as beneficial because it passed the responsibility for safety to the main Government health and safety regulator and away from the transport industry's representative government department. The privatisation of British Rail during the period of 1993 to 1996 saw a hundred companies taking charge of the rail industry. HSE introduced a new regulatory framework to manage the challenges to railway safety culture and risk management that took place during this period. The key components of the regulatory framework included new safety cases and permissioning regimes. From 1 April 2006 the Railway Inspectorate moved to the Office of Rail and Road (ORR).

HSE starts to carry out nuclear safety research

Responsibility for nuclear research passed from the
Department of Energy to the Health and Safety Commission
(HSC) on 1 April 1990. The Nuclear Safety Research
Management Unit (NSRMU) was established to manage the
nuclear safety research programme on behalf of HSC. Its
work was reviewed by the Advisory Committee on Safety
in Nuclear Installations' (ACSNI) Subcommittee on
Research. ACSNI was particularly concerned with the
reductions in nuclear research among the current nuclear
licensees due to commercial pressures, and consequently
stressed the need for HSC to support key areas of nuclear
research. ACSNI recommended that more research into the
effects of nuclear plant ageing, human factors and future
reactor designs would be beneficial. It also welcomed the
fact that HSC's research programme was being opened up
to competition and that customer-contractor arrangements
were being strengthened to ensure better targeting of
research priorities.

1991 HSE starts to enforce offshore safety

HSE's Offshore Division was established at the
recommendation of Lord Cullen's inquiry into the Piper
Alpha offshore explosion in 1988. This change in
responsibility brought about a shift in emphasis for the
industry, as prescriptive regulations which set specific
requirements on duty holders were replaced by goal-
setting regulations. One of the main requirements of the
new regime was the introduction of a safety case system in
which each installation is required to demonstrate that
major hazards are adequately controlled and that a
suitable management system is in place. Safety cases are
submitted to HSE for approval and approval must be
obtained before an offshore company is allowed to operate
on the UK continental shelf. Today's challenge for the
offshore industry and for HSE is to manage the integrity of

an ageing infrastructure while improving health and safety for the offshore workforce.

1992 'Six pack' regulations

Workplace (Health, Safety and Welfare) Regulations 1992 (S.I. 1992/3004)

The Regulations apply to the majority of workplaces and cover many workplace issues. These include: maintenance of workplaces and of equipment, devices and systems; ventilation; indoor workplace temperature; lighting; cleanliness and waste materials; room dimensions and space; workstations and seating; conditions of floors and traffic routes; falls or falling objects; windows and transparent / translucent doors, gates and walls; windows, skylights and ventilators; safe cleaning of windows; planning traffic routes; doors and gates; escalators and moving walkways; sanitary conveniences; washing facilities; drinking water; accommodation for clothing; and facilities for changing clothing, resting and eating meals.

Manual Handling Operations Regulations 1992 (S.I. 1992/2793)

The Regulations required employers to ensure 'so far as is reasonably practicable that employees should not be asked to carry out manual handling work where there is a risk of being injured'. Where such work is necessary, employers were required to make an assessment of the risks involved, take any appropriate steps required to ensure that risks are kept to a minimum, and provide employers undertaking such work with information about the weight of each load and the heaviest side of any load which has a non-centrally positioned centre of gravity. Schedule 1 of the Regulations outlined the factors that employers should take into account when carrying out an assessment of the risks associated with manual handling tasks.

ACORN SAFETY

The Health and Safety (Display Screen Equipment) Regulations 1992 (S.I. 1992/2792)

These Regulations require employers to assess all computer workstations to ensure health and safety risks are identified and effectively minimised. The Regulations stipulate that employees who use DSE in their work must be able to periodically take adequate breaks or changes of activity from using display screen equipment (DSE). Employees are also entitled to request eye and eyesight tests. Employers must also provide health and safety training and information about working with DSE to employees. The Regulations also set out requirements for display screens, keyboards, work desks or work surfaces and chairs as well as environmental factors such as providing adequate arrangements for space and lighting, along with measures for controlling noise, reflections and glare, heat, humidity and radiation. In addition, the software and tasks carried out by an operator or user of a computer must be appropriate to both the task being undertaken and the knowledge of the operator or user.

Provision and Use of Work Equipment Regulations 1992 (S.I. 1992/2932)

These Regulations, commonly known as PUWER, apply to the equipment provided for use in workplaces in general, including offshore installations. They also apply to self-employed people who use equipment in a work capacity. The Regulations impose a wide range of requirements for the provision and use of work equipment, including: suitability; maintenance; risks; information and instructions; training; EU conformity; dangerous parts of machinery; protection against specific hazards; working in high or very low temperatures; operating controls; isolation; stability; lighting; maintenance; markings; and warnings and exemptions.

Personal Protective Equipment at Work Regulations 1992 (S.I. 1992/2966)

The regulations stipulate that personal protective equipment (PPE) should be supplied and used in the workplace wherever there are risks to health and safety that cannot be eliminated or managed in any other way. The regulations also require that PPE is: properly assessed to ensure its suitability; issued with full instructions on its safe use; stored and maintained properly; and used correctly by employees.

The Management of Health and Safety at Work Regulations 1992 (S.I. 1992/2051)

The regulations set out responsibilities for carrying out risk assessments and health surveillance in the workplace, as well as putting health and safety arrangements including assistance in place. Other responsibilities set out by the regulations include: procedures for serious and imminent danger and for danger areas; co-operation and co-ordination between employers sharing work premises; self-employed persons' undertakings; working in hosted premises; providing information for employees; capabilities and training; employees' duties; and responsibilities towards temporary workers.

1993 150th anniversary of the Mines Inspectorate

HM Inspectorate of Mines was formed in 1843 under the leadership of Hugh Seymour Tremenheere. The mining industry has undergone many changes in the intervening years, but its safety record has improved tremendously and today the UK continues to be the world leader in mining health and safety.

ACORN SAFETY

1994 Construction (Design and Management) Regulations 1994 (S.I. 1994/3140)

The regulations were originally introduced in 1994 in compliance with European Directive 92/57/EEC. The Construction (Design and Management) Regulations 1994 (CDM) came into force on 31 March 1995. The first part of the Regulations dealt with the application of the Regulations and definitions. The second part outlined how the regulations apply to construction work. The roles and responsibilities of clients and agents of clients were explained in the third part. There were also separate sections for developers, appointments of principal contractor and planning supervisor and the responsibilities assigned to these roles.

Major Review of Regulation completed

In 1992, the Health and Safety Commission was charged with undertaking a review of extant health and safety legislation. The purpose of the review was to check whether existing legislation was still relevant and necessary in its current form. In addition, the review aimed to reduce the administrative burdens that legislation can place on small businesses and also examine HSE's general approach to enforcement. The review found that, while there was widespread support for the framework of health and safety legislation, much of the current law was seen as 'too voluminous, complicated and fragmented'. When the finding of the report was published in 1994, it recommended the removal of 100 sets of regulations and seven pieces of primary legislation as well as the simplification of many of the 340 requirements and recommendations for associated administrative paperwork. A comprehensive programme was put into place to achieve the necessary reforms and the ongoing process to reduce the burdens on business is described in HSE's Simplification Plan.

1995 100th anniversary of the Quarry Inspectorate

Health and Safety Laboratory (HSL) becomes an agency of HSE

An experimental station to investigate explosions in coal mines was set up at Eskmeals in Cumberland in 1911 by the UK government. Over the next few years, this area of research continued to grow and after the formation of the Safety in Mines Research Board in 1921, a site at Harpur Hill was acquired in 1924 for large scale mining safety work. The Safety in Mines Research Establishment (SMRE) was formed in 1947 and this combined the work of the Buxton site with the central laboratories which had opened in Sheffield in 1928. In 1959 the Occupational Medicine Laboratory was opened in London, and in 1975 the three organisations were merged to form the Health and Safety Executive's Research and Laboratory Services Division (RLSD) .RLSD's laboratories were integrated into one laboratory, the Health and Safety Laboratory, in 1995.

1996 Construction (Health, Safety and Welfare) Regulations 1996 (S.I. 1996/1592)

The Construction (Health, Safety and Welfare) Regulations 1996 came into force on 2nd September 1996. The Regulations set out a wide range of enforceable safety measures for the construction industry including the provision of "suitable and sufficient safe access to and egress from every place of work and to any other place provided for the use of any person while at work, which access and egress shall be without risks to health and properly maintained." Specific requirements of the Regulations included: preventing falls; ensuring the stability of structures; safe methods for demolition and dismantling operations; protection from falling objects; temperature and weather protection; fire detection and fire-fighting measures; provision of welfare facilities; safe use of explosives; provision of lighting; safe systems for using cofferdams and caissons; inspection by competent persons; training; and others.

1997 Southall rail accident

The Southall rail accident occurred when the 10.35 high speed train from Swansea to London Paddington collided with a freight train operated by English Welsh and Scottish Railway. The incident happened at 13.15 on 19 September 1997 at Southall East Junction. Seven people died in the accident and 139 people were injured, some of these sustaining serious injuries. HSE's Railway Inspectorate investigated the incident and an official inquiry was conducted by Professor John Uff.

1998 Gas Safety (Installation and Use) Regulations 1998 (S.I. 1998/2451)

The first of the general provisions of the Regulations covered qualification and supervision and states that 'No person shall carry out work in relation to a gas fitting or gas storage vessel unless he is competent to do so'. The Regulations imposed a duty on employers to ensure that people carrying out work on gas installations have been approved by HSE under regulation 3(3) of these Regulations. Requirements for materials and workmanship, protection against damage, existing gas fittings as well as general safety precautions are also outlined in the Regulations.

1999 40th anniversary of the Nuclear Installation Inspectorate

The Nuclear Installations Inspectorate (NII) came into being in 1959, under one of the provisions of the Nuclear Installations Act 1959. The Act came into force as a consequence of the Fleck Inquiry into the fire at Windscale

Pile 1. This incident which occurred in 1957 has been the UK's worst nuclear accident to date. Over the years, NII has been involved in responding to accidents such as Three Mile Island and Chernobyl, participating in major public inquiries and providing help to European regulators. Today's Nuclear Directorate (ND) sets the safety and security standards to be used on nuclear sites in the UK. ND is also involved in a Transition Programme aimed at creating a new Nuclear Statutory Corporation (NSC) that will incorporate all elements of the HSE's Nuclear Directorate (Nuclear Installations Directorate, Office for Civil Nuclear Security and UK Safeguards Office).

Control of Major Accident Hazards Regulations 1999 (S.I. 1999/743)

The Control of Major Accident Hazards Regulations 1999 (COMAH) set out the responsibilities of operators of plants where scheduled hazardous chemicals are used, to prevent major accidents and limit the consequences of major accidents to people and the environment. The regulations require operators to formulate a major accident prevention policy and also to notify the competent authority at the start of the construction of a plant handling scheduled chemicals and at the end, when the plant is being decommissioned or the chemicals are no longer present on site. The regulations also require detailed safety reports to be sent to the competent authority and for operators to produce emergency plans in consultation with local authorities. In addition, operators must provide information to the public with regard to local safety measures and actions to take in the event of a major accident at a COMAH site.

Ladbroke Grove train crash (31 fatalities)

Thirty-one people died and over 400 were injured when a passenger train passed a red signal and collided with a high-speed passenger train at Ladbroke Grove in West London on 5 October 1999. The Health and Safety Executive's Railway Inspectorate investigated the incident and Lord Cullen chaired a Public Inquiry into the causes of the crash as well as wider issues relating to regulatory matters and safety management. In 2004 HSE won a prosecution against Thames Trains for breaches of Section 2 and 3 of the Health and Safety at Work etc Act relating to driver training. Following this, in 2005, the Crown Prosecution Service successfully prosecuted Network Rail Infrastructure (formerly Railtrack Plc) under Section 3 of the Health and Safety at Work etc Act.

Bill Callaghan appointed as Chair of the Health and Safety Commission

Bill Callaghan took up the post of Chair of the Health and Safety Commission in October 1999. Formerly the Chief Economist and Head of the Economic and Social Affairs Department at the Trades Union Congress (TUC), Bill Callaghan also served on the Low Pay Commission from 1997 – 2000. During his time as HSC Chair, Bill Callaghan played a major role in the 'Revitalising Health and Safety' campaign which set targets and priorities for improving health and safety performance. He also led on the development of HSC's strategy to 2010 and beyond and spearheaded the sensible risk campaign which was aimed at overturning health and safety myths. Bill Callaghan was knighted in June 2007 in recognition of his outstanding contribution to health and safety management at work. He also received a Distinguished Service Award from the Royal Society for the Prevention of Accidents (RoSPA) in October of that year.

2000 'Revitalising Health and Safety strategy' launched

The Revitalising Health and Safety Strategy Statement was published in June 2000 to mark the start of the ten-year campaign of the same name. The Revitalising Health and Safety strategy was launched at a time when the same proportion of people had been injured at work since the early 1990s. The aim of the Revitalising Health and Safety strategy was to help people at work to protect themselves and their business, to improve the quality of life in the workplace and to help employers and employees to make work safer and healthier. Measurable targets were set and reviewed at regular intervals.

'Securing health together occupational health strategy for Great Britain' launched

The 'Securing health together occupational health strategy for Great Britain' was launched in 2000 as a ten-year strategy for reducing high levels of occupational ill-health and the resulting costs to families, employers and society. The Strategy was based on several main targets: to reduce ill health in workers and the public that had been caused or affected by work; to help people who had been ill to return to work, whether or not their work had caused their absence; to improve work opportunities for people not in work due to illness or disability; to use the work environment to help people improve or maintain their health. A number of measurable targets were at the heart of the Strategy and the contemporary estimated gross benefits of reaching the targets were estimated to be 6.6 to 21.8 billion pounds sterling by 2010.

2004 HSC's 'Strategy for workplace health and safety to 2010 and beyond' launched

A Strategy was launched in February 2004 to set a new direction for the role of the Health and Safety Commission, Health and Safety Executive and Local Authorities. The Strategy aimed to improve poor safety performances, engender a greater participation of workers in workplace health and safety, build closer involvement between stakeholders and HSE, and provide clearer and simple information and advice in a more accessible way.

Morecambe Bay: death of cockle-pickers (21 fatalities)

An incident occurred on the night of 5-6 February 2004 when 35 cockle pickers, most of whom were Chinese, were cut off by the tide as they worked on the cockle banks on Morecambe Bay. It is thought that 23 of the workers died, although only 21 bodies were recovered. HSE inspectors joined with the police in a major investigation into the incident. The Crown Prosecution Service brought criminal charges of manslaughter and facilitation against a number of individuals. Following the incident, HSE produced some practical guidelines for safe working in tidal areas and estuaries. Some organisers of cockling work also introduced some improvements to their work processes, including: providing protective clothing and high-visibility garments; using better vehicles; and carrying dinghies, lifejackets and life rafts.

HSE's Infoline service received its 2 millionth call

The HSE Infoline public enquiry contact centre took its two millionth call in September 2004. Run by the National Britannia Group based in Caerphilly, Infoline was set up in July 1996 to provide health and safety information and access to expert sources of guidance and advice. While Infoline's services are available to anyone with an interest in workplace health and safety matters, the majority of enquiries come from small and medium-sized enterprises (SMEs). Enquirers can remain anonymous if they wish and all enquiries are treated confidentially. The most common queries relate to asbestos, the Reporting of Injuries, Diseases and Dangerous Occurrences Regulations (RIDDOR) and health and safety requirements for setting up a new business.
[Update: In a move to improve efficiency further and deliver value for taxpayers, HSE's Infoline ended on 30 September 2011.

Explosion at ICL Plastic factory, Maryhill, Glasgow

An explosion occurred at the ICL Plastics factory in Maryhill, Glasgow, on 11 May 2004. Nine people were killed in the incident and many more suffered injuries. The explosion occurred when liquefied petroleum gas (LPG) leaked from an underground metal pipe in the basement of the factory. The LPG ignited and the resulting explosion caused the building to collapse.

Lord Brian Gill was appointed to hold an Inquiry into the events that led up to the disaster. HSE inspectors and retired inspectors and the Chief Executive and the then Deputy Chief Executive gave evidence in the formal hearings. Lord Gill's report was published in July 2009 and

outlined various recommendations for HSE as the body
which (together with Local Authorities) regulates LPG
hazards in industrial and commercial premises.

2005 Buncefield explosion

A series of explosions occurred at the Buncefield Oil
Storage Depot at Hemel Hempstead in Hertfordshire on
11th December 2005. A large area of the site was engulfed
by a fire which resulted from one of the initial massive
explosions. Although more than 50 people were injured in
the incident, no-one died. A large area around the
Buncefield site was evacuated as a precaution. Many of the
commercial and residential properties in the vicinity were
damaged in the incident. The fire, which burned for several
days, destroyed most of the site and released large plumes
of black smoke into the atmosphere. The Health and Safety
Executive and the Environment Agency launched a joint
investigation into the incident. Five companies were
prosecuted as a result of the incident. A series of
recommendations from HSE was published under the title
"Recommendations on land use planning and the control of
societal risk around major hazard sites" and the
investigation culminated in the publication of the final
report in December 2008.

2006 Transfer of responsibility for railway safety from HSE to the Office of the Rail Regulator

HSE assumed responsibility for railway safety in 1990
when the Railway Inspectorate moved from the
Department of Transport. The move took place following
criticism of the Inspectorate for not protecting passengers
adequately and for not using modern risk assessment
techniques. During the period 1993 to 1996, British Rail
was privatised and over a hundred companies took charge
of the railways. This resulted in a major change to railway
safety culture and risk management. HSE introduced a new

regulatory framework to manage these changes and the key elements of the framework included new safety case and permissioning regimes. On 1 April 2006 railway safety passed to the Office of Rail and Road (ORR).

Workplace Health Connect launched

Workplace Health Connect was launched in February 2006 as a two-year pilot project to give advice on workplace health, safety and return to work issues. The advice given by the pilot was free, confidential and practical and was aimed at small and medium sized businesses (i.e. those with between 5 and 250 workers) in England and Wales. Workplace Connect was managed, funded and quality controlled by HSE but was independently run. It incorporated an Adviceline, a problem-solving visit service and a system of referrals to approved local specialists where appropriate. The pilot ended in February 2008.

Redgrave Court new headquarters officially opened

HSE's new headquarters building, Redgrave Court, based in Bootle, Merseyside, was officially opened by HRH the Duke of York on 19 July 2006. Redgrave Court has provided a central base for staff and contractors who previously occupied six separate buildings. It has enabled staff to undertake new and more efficient ways of working, allowed for better use of resources, and provided increased access to senior managers.

2007 Responsibility for the Adventure Activities Licensing Authority (AALA) passes to HSE

The Adventure Activities Licensing Authority (AALA) was launched in 1996 and became HSE's responsibility in 2007. The AALA controls the licensing regime for the provision of adventure activities for young people within the scope of the Adventure Activities Licensing Regulations 2004

ACORN SAFETY

(AALR). HSE's Field Operations and Policy Group work with organisations in this sector to provide guidance, advice and support and to improve health and safety.

Construction (Design and Management) Regulations (CDM 2007) (S.I. 2007/320) launched

The CDM Regulations combine the CDM Regulations 1994 and the Construction (Health, Safety and Welfare) Regulations 1996 into one regulatory package, aimed at alleviating the previously complex and at times, bureaucratic approach taken by many duty holders. The aim of the CDM Regulations is to reduce the risk of harm to workers who build, use, maintain and demolish structures. Effective planning and management of construction projects, from design concept onwards, is at the heart of the Regulations. The aim is for health and safety considerations to be treated as a normal part of a project's development, not an afterthought or bolt-on extra.

Bill Callaghan is knighted for his services to health and safety

Bill Callaghan became Chair of the Health and Safety Commission (HSC) on 1 October 1999. During his career with HSC and HSE, Bill Callaghan championed the sensible risk message, had a leading role in ensuring that risks to health and safety in the workplace are properly controlled and has played a key role in developing the HSC/E Strategy to 2010. In 2007, Bill Callaghan was knighted for his services to health and safety. He left HSE on 27 Sept 2007 and was replaced by Judith E. Hackitt CBE.

Judith Hackitt appointed as new Chair of the Health and Safety Commission, following on from the retirement of Sir Bill Callaghan

Judith Hackitt was appointed as Chair of the Health and Safety Commission (HSC) on 1 October 2007. Ms Hackitt's five year appointment followed on from her previous role as a Commissioner of HSC during the period 2002 – 2005 and an assignment as Director of the European Chemical Industry Council's Chemistry for Europe project.

HSE takes on responsibility for the security activities of the Office for Nuclear Security (OCNS) and UK Safeguards Office (UKSO)

On 1 April 2007 the security activities of the Office for Civil Nuclear Security (OCNS) transferred to the Health and Safety Executive. This happened as a result of recommendations in the 2005 Hampton report. This means that HSE's Nuclear Directorate became the single point of contact for operational matters relating to nuclear safety, security and safeguards. You can find out more about the work of OCNS from HSE's Nuclear Directorate web pages.

ACORN SAFETY

The Registration, Evaluation, Authorisation and Restriction of Chemicals (REACH) European Union regulations come into force in the UK and across Europe

The Registration, Evaluation, Authorisation and Restriction of Chemicals (REACH) Regulations came into force on 1 June 2007, replacing several Regulations and European directives with a single system. One of the main requirements of REACH is for importers or manufacturers of substances to register them with the central European Chemicals Agency. The aim of this is to ensure that human health and the environment is protected by ensuring that manufacturers and importers understand and manage the risks associated with chemicals. REACH also allows substances to move freely on the EU market as well as allowing for free competition and innovation in the European chemicals industry.

Responsibility for the Adventure Licensing Authority (AALA) passes to HSE

2008 HSC/HSE merges to form one organisation

The Health and Safety Commission and Health and Safety Executive took the decision to merge their powers and functions to become a new unitary body with the name 'Health and Safety Executive'. The merger took place following a 2006 consultation exercise setting out the benefits of the merger.

Health and Safety (Offences) Act 2008

The Health and Safety (Offences) Act 2008 came into force on 16 January 2009. Under the provisions of the Act, offenders who break the law will be subjected to higher fines and longer sentences. The Act makes imprisonment an option for more health and safety offences in both the lower and higher courts. It also allows certain offences, which at one time could only be tried in lower courts, to be tried in the higher courts. However, the main change which the Act has brought is to raise the maximum fine which may be imposed in the lower courts to £20,000 for most health and safety offences.

Pesticides Safety Directorate transfers to HSE

The Pesticides Safety Directorate (PSD) transferred from the Department for Environment, Food and Rural Affairs (Defra) to HSE on 1 April 2008 following recommendations of the 2005 Hampton Review of Regulators. The transfer allowed PSD and HSE to explore joint areas of interest for example on regulatory science and policy for chemicals, pesticides, detergents and biocides. PSD has retained a distinct identity in HSE and continues to have its policy set by Defra.

2009 Gas Safe Register - 10-year contract to Capita

A new registration scheme for gas engineers was launched on 1 April 2009. The scheme is known as the Gas Safe Register and is administered under a 10-year contract by the Capita Group Plc. Under the Gas Safe Register, Capita have made a commitment to deliver improvements to gas safety by raising awareness of domestic gas risks among consumers and by increasing public confidence in registered gas engineers and the safety of public gas work. Gas engineers will also benefit from the Gas Safe Register as they will have more flexible payment and registration options. The administrative burdens on them will also be reduced.

Health and safety law poster replaced - after 10 years' service!

A new version of the health and safety law poster was published on 6 April 2009. The poster includes a list of basic points relating to health and safety in the workplace and it outlines what employers and workers must do to comply with the law. The health and safety poster must be displayed in all workplaces or if this is not possible, each employee must be given a copy of the leaflet version.

HSE launches strategy for the health and safety of GB

HSE's new Strategy was launched in 2009 following the aim of the new 2008 Board to develop a 'renewed momentum to improve health and safety performance.' One of the key drivers for this is the fact that the combined rate of illness and injury in Great Britain is the same as it was in 2004. The Board wanted to build on existing strengths, develop new ways of engaging with the workforce and meet continuing challenges for health and safety. The Strategy explains that everyone has a role to play in improving health and safety in the workplace but there must be strong leadership and commitment to drive this forward. Training is described as a key component of the improvement process. The Strategy also reinforces HSE's role in inspection and enforcement along with monitoring hazardous industries to guard against possible catastrophes.

2010 Health and Safety Pledge Forum launched

The Health and Safety Pledge Forum was launched on 24 February 2010 as part of HSE's 2009 Strategy: The Health and Safety of Great Britain\\ Be part of the solution. The Strategy encouraged organisations to show their commitment to workplace health and safety by signing the HSE Safety Pledge. HSE is keen for those who have signed the Pledge to share ideas for improving health and safety with each other or to work with HSE on collaborative ventures in risk management. The Pledge Forum helps this process by allowing pledge signers to share ideas and best practice and ask questions. It also contains a wealth of information on a range of topics, including: worker protection; absence management; saving recruitment and insurance costs; improving productivity; reputation management; and case studies for both small/medium sized businesses and large businesses.

HSE introduces new Safety Alerts

In 2010 HSE revised its Safety Bulletin system to improve the way it warns industry about problems with substances, equipment, procedures and processes that may cause injury. The information contained in the bulletins is gathered from a range of sources including inspections, research, investigations, advice from industry and the EU Commission. There are three types of bulletin: Alerts which are immediate and vital; Notice which do not require immediate action but must be dealt with within a given timescale; and Other information which needs to be shared with a wide audience or specific group or sector of industry. Safety Bulletins can be received via email, text message or RSS feed and are also available on the HSE Website.

The Control of Artificial Optical Radiation at Work Regulations 2010 (S.I. 2010/1140)

The Control of Artificial Optical Radiation at Work Regulations 2010 aim to protect workers from health risks associated with exposure to hazardous sources of artificial optical radiation (AOR). The Regulations require employers who may expose workers to AOR to assess the risk of adverse health effects of AOR to the skin or eyes. This assessment should include measurements or calculations for the levels of radiation to which employees are exposed. It must also assess the level, wavelength and duration of exposure. Employers are required to reduce or eliminate exposure to AOR where practicable, provide appropriate information and training for employees, and ensure that exposed employees have their health monitored and receive medical examinations. HSE has produced 'Guidance for Employers on the Control of Artificial Optical Radiation at Work Regulations (AOR) 2010' for those employers who would like to find out more about their responsibilities under the Regulations.

Lord Young's review of health and safety, 'Common Sense – Common Safety' is published

Lord Young's report was published on 15 October 2010 and sets out a series of recommendations for improving the way health and safety is applied in Great Britain and for reviewing today's 'compensation culture'. The review, commissioned by the then Prime Minister, David Cameron, has a wider remit than HSE's sphere of responsibility, however HSE has welcomed Lord Young's review and has continued to offer information and participate in improvements where appropriate. To this end, HSE has co-operated with a number of organisations to develop the Occupational Safety Consultants Register (OSCR). This will go live in January 2011. HSE has also produced a series of risk assessment tools for offices, shops, classrooms and charity shops.

2011 Occupational Safety Consultants Register (OSHCR)

The Occupational Safety Consultants Register (OSHCR) provides a source for identifying consultants who are qualified to provide general advice on health and safety to help UK businesses manage workplace risks. While many companies will feel confident about carrying out their own workplace risk assessments and implementing appropriate health and safety measures, those who need additional help can turn to OSHCR. The consultants listed in OSHCR are recognised by the key occupational health and safety organisations who participate in the OSHCR scheme. OSHCR can be used to search for consultants by keyword, industry, topic, county, or by provision of free information.

The Office for Nuclear Regulation (ONR) launched 1 April

On 1 April 2011, the Office for Nuclear Regulation (ONR) was established as an agency of the Health and Safety Executive. ONR's objective is to consolidate the functions of HSE's Nuclear Directorate including the Nuclear Installations Inspectorate, the Office for Civil Nuclear Security and the UK Safeguards Office, as well as the Department for Transport's Radioactive Materials Transport Division. ONR is responsible for protecting people from the hazards inherent in the nuclear industry. It does this through enforcing relevant legislation and by encouraging the nuclear industry to aspire to an exemplary health and safety culture. ONR uses specialist advice from HSE and consultants and runs a nuclear safety studies programme to help it with inspection and assessment work. It also provides specialist assistance to various international energy organisations as well as nuclear regulators in a range of countries.

HSL celebrates 100 years

The Health and Safety Laboratory (HSL) celebrated its centenary in 2011. HSL is a leading scientific health and safety research organisation specialising in work-related activities. It is based in Buxton and its origins can be traced back to a 1911 Government-funded initiative aimed at investigating explosions in coal mines. The Safety in Mines Research Board was formed 10 years later, and its work was conducted in both Buxton and Sheffield. Over the next few years the Buxton site became the Explosion and Flame Laboratory while the Sheffield site focussed on safety engineering. The Occupational Medicine and Hygiene Laboratory in Cricklewood, North London, joined the existing research teams in 1966. In 1995 the three laboratories were combined together to form HSL, as an agency of HSE. HSL moved to Buxton in 2004.

Löfstedt report published

Professor Ragnar Löfstedt's report: 'Reclaiming health and safety for all: an independent review of health and safety legislation' was published in November 2011. The report was commissioned by Employment Minister Chris Grayling as part of the Government's plan to overhaul the health and safety system in Britain. The report considers ways in which health and safety legislation can be combined, simplified or reduced so that the burden on British businesses can be alleviated. At the same time, it suggests how progress in improving health and safety in the workplace can continue. The report takes into account the views of employers' and employees' organisations, Government bodies, academics and professional health and safety organisations.

2012 The Control of Asbestos Regulations 2012 (S.I. 2012/632) launched

The Regulations came into force in April 2012 and updated earlier asbestos regulations to take account of the fact that in the European Commission's view, the UK had not completely implemented the EU Directive on exposure to asbestos as set out in EU Directive 2009/148/EC). The changes brought about by the new Regulations are fairly small and mostly affect some types of non-licensed work with asbestos including medical surveillance, record keeping and notification of work.

Fee for Intervention (FFI) launched 1 October

HSE's new cost recovery scheme known as Fee for Intervention (FFI) came into force on 1 October 2012. FFI is administered under the Health and Safety (Fees) Regulations 2012 and is used to recover HSE's costs against those who contravene health and safety laws. The costs that are recouped in this way are those for inspection, investigation and taking enforcement action. FFI is designed to ensure that companies who break health and safety laws quickly put matters right. It will also discourage companies who try to undercut their competitors by flouting health and safety laws and putting people at risk.

2013 The Health and Safety (Sharp Instruments in Healthcare) Regulations (S.I. 2013/645)

The Health and Safety (Sharp Instruments in Healthcare) Regulations 2013 (S.I. 2013/645) which came into effect on 11 May 2013, require employers to ensure that the risks from needles and other 'sharps' used in healthcare are effectively controlled. The regulations stipulate that healthcare employers and contractors must provide suitable arrangements for the safe use and disposal of sharps and must train workers to understand the risks. In addition, the Regulations require employers and contactors to investigate any work-related incidents involving sharps, and to take appropriate action.

Health and Safety (Miscellaneous Repeals, Revocations and Amendments) Regulations 2013 (S.I. 2013/448)

The Health and Safety (Miscellaneous Repeals, Revocations and Amendments) Regulations 2013 (S.I. 2013/448) came into force on 6 April 2013. These Regulations are designed to revoke a series of redundant and / or out of date legislation, including one Act and twelve statutory instruments. HSE has introduced these Regulations as part of a process of ensuring that employers can quickly understand their duty to provide a safe and healthy working environment for employees.

Construction (Design and Management) Regulations 2015 (S.I. 2014/3248)

The Construction (Design and Management) Regulations 2015 (CDM 2015) came into force on 6 April 2015, replacing CDM 2007.

These regulations offer a very broad definition of what construction works are. Everyone involved in a construction project, including home maintenance and improvement works, holds responsibility for health and safety.

The regulations now apply to all clients of construction projects, whether or not a person is acting in the course or furtherance of a business.

Pre-construction archaeological investigations are not included within the scope of the definition of construction work.

The role of CDM coordinator was removed and various duties have been recast including client duties and general duties.

A client is required to appoint a principal designer as well as a principal contractor in any project where there is, or it is reasonably foreseeable that there will be, more than one contractor working on the project.

Under the 2007 Regulations, appointments for similar roles were required for notifiable projects. The duty to notify now lies with a client and the threshold for notification is raised.

The scope of what constitutes 'construction work' has been increased. 'Construction work' now means the carrying out of any building, civil engineering or engineering construction work and includes building temporary structures used for events, television, film and entertainment productions.

2020 COVID 19 Pandemic

In 2020 the COVID-19 pandemic hit the UK and the HSE released several guidance notes in quick succession on things such as PPE, RPE, social distancing and cleaning and hygiene.

CHAPTER 3

Dreaded Government Regulations

The boring but needed bit

In the UK, there is a hierarchy of Health and Safety Legislation, which has an umbrella type effect that cascades down the chain to the next.

The hierarchy looks like this:

ACTS OF PARLIAMENT

REGULATIONS

APPROVED CODE OF PRACTICE

HEALTH AND SAFETY GUIDANCE NOTES

DUTYHOLDER

Act of Parliament

An act is the primary piece of legislation. An Act of Parliament must be passed through and agreed upon by Parliament itself.

It also must receive consent from the Queen and only passes as law once it has received both nods of approval. Acts therefore usually take a very long time to bring to fruition.

Regulations

Regulations are known as secondary legislation. Regulations are not require to be passed by Parliament and the Queen.

Acts of Parliament give ministers the power to make Regulations within a particular area under the Act.

Regulations require the same sort of compliance. However, they can be introduced much faster than Acts of Parliament themselves.

Approved Codes of Practice

Approved Codes of Practice, also known as ACoPs, are the recommended or preferred methods or standards that are required to be met.

The ACoPs are written to be in line with the main Regulations and Acts.

By order of following in line with the ACoPs, the Regulations and Acts will also be complied with. They provide insight and guides to what is expected and what is meant in the Regulations and Acts. They provide information such as what is deemed "reasonably practicable".

Reasonably practicable is a term the industry loves to use. If you're familiar with any health and safety guidance documents, we're sure you will have come across it before. The dictionary meanings for both words are...

Reasonably – to a moderate or acceptable degree.

Practicable – able to be done or put into practice successfully.

In the health and safety world, reasonably practicable usually implies that the "owner" must make a calculation where the scale of risk is measured against what is required in averting that risk.

RISK
COST, TIME, TROUBLE

In simple terms, think of a scale. On one side is the risk and on the other side is cost, time and trouble to reduce or eliminate the risk. The owner must do as much as possible to tip the scale in favour of eliminating the risk.

Health and Safety Guidance Notes

Health and Safety Guidance Notes are written to interpret what the law states. This interpretation helps the reader to comply with the law.

They also provide technical advice and information and can also prescribe elements of how some items must be completed.

All the HSE documents can be purchased from the Health and Safety Executives book publishing arm. This is the link to the HSE website: **www.hse.gov.uk**

Alternatively, the documents can also be downloaded for free from the same link.

The PDF versions cover the same material but are laid out slightly differently and also have fewer photos and illustrations within them. The PDF versions are great.

The content pages hyperlink to the relevant pages and you can search for keywords, which makes these documents easier to use.

As they're electronic, you can keep the full library of documents on your desktop, laptop, tablet or phone.

It's worthwhile noting that although the documents can be downloaded or purchased from the HSE website, in fact, some of the information held within is now out of date and incorrect!

One of the obvious ones is the references to the CAWR Regulations, which were the old Control of Asbestos at Work Regulations – these are wholly superseded by the CAR 2012 (Control of Asbestos Regulations 2012).

There are other changes within these documents also.

CHAPTER 4

Appointed Competent Health and Safety Person

Why most people need one

S0, we now know that health and safety isn't something new, it's quite complex and if we don't comply then it can cost in more ways than one.

Now, the layout of having this here before we tell you what's actually needed in place might seem backwards.

However, it's here now so it's up front for you to consider. I don't want you reading this book thinking that once this book's inside your brain you can go off and simply solve every health and safety issue you have on your own. You can't I'm afraid, it's not as simple as that and I'll have you consider that the only solution to solving the H&S puzzle is to work with your own retained consultant. Please let me explain further below.

The term "Appointed Competent Person for health and safety" gets banded about quite a bit in and around the industry, but what does this actually mean for you?

Well, the long and short of it is that if you have five or more employees then legally you must appoint a competent person to assist you with your legal obligations.

Five or more employees? Legally you must appoint a competent person.

But the kicker is, if you're sitting at 4 people in your business I'm afraid it's not the Wild West, you can't just crack on and ignore the government regulations, they still apply, and you still have to do and have certain things in place.

So, what is a competent person?

The Health and Safety Executive state a competent person to be:

"A competent person is someone who has sufficient training and experience or knowledge and other qualities that allow them to assist you properly "

Now, most businesses up to a certain level simply do not have those resources in house and cannot afford to employ someone to undertake this role. This means that they are at risk from all the things mentioned in previous chapters. So, what other options do you have seeing that sticking your head in the sand and hoping for the best isn't one!?

A) Go it alone
B) Employ a H&S expert in house
C) Employ a H&S expert contractor
D) Work together with a retained consultant

The answer for most people is D and you'll soon see why.

A) Go it alone

So, you're a fully qualified health and safety expert with years under your belt, congratulations! By all means go it alone.

However, I'm guessing you're not, right? Don't get me wrong you're definitely better positioned and doing more than most by reading this book right now.

I'm guessing that you may have a bit of H&S experience but don't have the qualifications and experience to fully back up what you want to achieve.

And that's exactly it. Unless you're actually doing the job for a living you can't prove competence. Competence is the key driver to proving that what we've done was fair enough in times when things go wrong. You'll need to prove that in a court of law.

This is why going it alone is never an option for anyone unless they are a trained Health and Safety consultant.

B) Employ a H&S expert in house

On the face of it, this may seem the easiest and simplest solution to your needs. However, proceed with caution for a few reasons.

The first has got to be the cost. A good health and safety manager does not come cheap. They will need the full skillset to understand what you do as a business, what risks are involved, how you run, and where your business is going.

Their package is likely to run into the tens of thousands because of their skillset and package required (phone, laptop, car, expenses etc).

That's even if you can actually find one that suits you. Most businesses even in a very generic industry have their own way of doing things, so to find someone who fits in with your culture and how you do things can be an absolute minefield. There are also the issues surrounding employing another person and overhead at your company which can upset people, ruffle feathers and who knows what they will actually turn out like because if they bring baggage or start going off sick it can be a huge pain to deal with getting rid and finding someone new.

C) Employ a H&S expert contractor

Again, this could seem a good way to go on the face of it but let's dig a little deeper.

There are lots of one-man band health and safety consultants out there that tout themselves as one size fits all. This is not usually the case because to be completely up to date and current across all health and safety fields is some feat.

You see, the world of health and safety is constantly moving and goalposts are changing. Not only from what's handed down by Government with laws and regulation changes but also from what's expected from clients - especially larger firms that you may do business for. You see, it's not just about ensuring you're doing your bit for your people, it's also about ensuring you're meeting the requirements from any of your clients.

The thing with the laws and regulations is that they are essentially a minimum requirement. There's no stopping people asking for more than what the regulations state.

This means that you can come unstuck when tendering for new work or even doing work because they make up their own rules on what meets their requirements with regards to skillset, qualifications, and accreditations.

Employing a one man band usually means that you forgo a level of skill that you may need and you also forgo the backup of having accreditations proving that you and your company are deemed fully competent.

There is also a level of uncertainty out there in the marketplace, especially in climates such as now. This means that the one-man band consultants easily fall in and out of work until they can't sustain their financial needs, and have to go and get a job which leaves you in the lurch.

Or, they charge you the money and seem to be doing everything for you however because of the climate and market place they actually take on too many clients to keep their figures up but then you don't get what you're paying for as they are spreading themselves too thinly.

This again can leave you in the lurch and not fully protected from the onslaught of health and safety regelation which we know is not what you want.

If you do any works on any sites

D) Work together with a retained consultant

Out of the three options this is the most viable one for most people in your position, however you still need to be cautious so that you get what you need.

There are a lot of firms out in the market touting a one size fits all approach, but this doesn't necessarily provide you with what you need either. You need bespoke health and safety because unless it's fit for purpose it's no good. In fact, you may as well not bother and save up the money for the fine and court case that will come your way.

There are however companies that can provide this correctly. If you carefully select your health and safety company, you can get to that nirvana of having no issues with health and safety when they come knocking.

There are a few things to look out for when selecting a company. Like previously mentioned you will need a bespoke service that works for you from a consultant that has the necessary experience. When selecting a company, identify who will be your actual person to deal with because it's usually not the shiny salesperson you meet or hear at the end of the phone promising you the earth.

There are a few reasons you need to identify who will be your contact. You need to see their CV; you need to be sure that they do have the skillset to meet your needs.

The second thing is that you need to know you get along. You see, the problem with a lot of H&S bods is that they are very H&S orientated which is great but it means that they are rigid and there is no room for discussion with how you do things.

Their approach is very much "my way or the highway", with a very singular view of the world. This is no good because you will need to work together and need to have that relationship of trust and partnership. That's the only way true health and safety gets rolled out properly. If it's just a bit of paper and isn't how you actually do things then again there's no point in having it, and also working with someone who rubs you up the wrong way will only get your back up and make you hate H&S more than you probably do already!

Some top tips for finding a retained consultant you can work with:

- Check your consultant has the skillset you need, ask for references and proof

- Ensure they understand your business and how you work, that's the only way to get real advice

- Be sure that documents produced are not off the shelf rubbish, again it needs to work and fit in with your company

- Find out how they plan to keep you up to date, you want a consultant with their ear to the ground so you can stay ahead of the curve

- Make sure they have decent accreditations; this helps in the long run with proving that they are indeed competent

- They should have a H&S system that doesn't cost you anything. In this day and age online systems and storage are cheap enough and you shouldn't be paying for ongoing costs for access to that. There should be free unlimited storage and you should be able to access the system 24/7

If you follow these tips then you are sure to find a retained consultant that you can work with, and you will find that the health and safety journey is one that actually benefits your business rather than it being just a tick box exercise.

CHAPTER 5

Reasonably Practicable, Hazard and Risk

What do these terms actually mean?

T
o fully comply with health and safety law we need to understand some of the basic concepts and terms that are used.

Reasonably Practicable, Hazard and Risk are often used and they can definitely be confusing, so in the next few paragraphs I hope to clear these terms up in what they mean to the HSE, what they mean to you, and what consequences they carry if misunderstood.

"Reasonably Practicable"

Reasonably practicable is banded about often when discussing health and safety and complying with the law, but what does it actually mean? I'll shine a light on it and explain it in the next few paragraphs.

You may have also heard other similar terms such as "ALARP" or "SFAIRP". "ALARP" is an acronym or abbreviation for "as low as reasonably practicable". "SFAIRP" is an acronym or abbreviation for "so far as is reasonably practicable". The two terms basically mean the same thing, and this is where the concept of "reasonably practicable" comes from and sits at their core.

But let's be honest, it all just sounds like legal speak and it doesn't exactly roll off the tongue easily does it!?

The HSE's version of what it means is: *"Weighing a risk against the trouble, time and money needed to control it"*. In practicality it means have you done enough to look after people that could be affected or not?

The HSE give two extreme examples but they actually get the point across very well and provide a clearer picture of the term:

- *To spend £1m to prevent five staff suffering bruised knees is obviously grossly disproportionate; but*

- *To spend £1m to prevent a major explosion capable of killing 150 people is obviously proportionate.*

The HSE say that the use of this term and other similar ones as mentioned above essentially all meaning the same thing requires judgement when deciding if something fits because in reality nothing is ever that obvious or that simple.

The term is used as a yardstick for what the HSE expect to see. The way HSE use it is to set goals for duty holders to comply with, more of a holistic approach rather than being totally prescriptive in what is required. In their own admission this approach has its advantages but also has drawbacks because it requires judgement from both parties.

A lot of the time however it also takes into consideration industry good practices and what everyone else is generally doing in a similar situation. But for more complex situations, the HSE will use other more formal decision-making tools such as cost-benefit analysis.

Hazard or Risk?

The following explanation has been taken directly from the HSE and how they determine these words:

Definition of a hazard

A hazard is something (e.g. an object, a property of a substance, a phenomenon, or an activity) that can cause adverse effects. For example:

- *Water on a staircase is a hazard because you could slip on it, fall and hurt yourself.*

- *Loud noise is a hazard because it can cause hearing loss.*

- *Breathing in asbestos dust is a hazard because it can cause cancer.*

So basically speaking, the hazard is the "thing" that may cause an issue either instantly or at a later point in time.

Definition of a risk

A risk is the likelihood that a hazard will actually cause its adverse effects, together with a measure of the effect. It is a two-part concept and you have to have both parts to make sense of it. Likelihoods can be expressed as probabilities (e.g. "one in a thousand"), frequencies (e.g. "1,000 cases per year") or in a qualitative way (e.g. "negligible", "significant", etc.). The effect can be described in many different ways. For example:

- The annual risk of a worker in Great Britain experiencing a fatal accident [effect] at work [hazard] is less than one in 100,000 [likelihood];

- About 1,500 workers each year [likelihood] in Great Britain suffer a non-fatal major injury [effect] from contact with moving machinery [hazard]; or

- The lifetime risk of an employee developing asthma [effect] from exposure to substance X [hazard] is significant [likelihood].

So again, basically speaking, the risk is the likelihood of the thing actually causing its adverse effect.

So hopefully you now know and understand some of the terms that are thrown about in health and safety, and this should make it easier to comply with the core principles and have the knowledge of the core concepts of what's required.

CHAPTER 6

What do you need in place?

The core basics needed

N ow we know what health and safety is about and some of the history, but what do you actually need?

As I alluded to in the last chapter most people choose to get support from an appointed health and safety expert so that they know they are fully covered and are not open to falling foul of the Government regulations.

But let's take a look at what the majority of businesses need in place to comply with the standard regulations. Now, for other complex businesses or tasks there will be a ream of other requirements needed to be in place so that you are complying with the law, but this at least gives you a good idea of what's needed generally and what's considered best practice.

Under law as an employer it is your duty as in you are responsible to protect the health, safety and welfare of your employees and also other people that might be affected by your business. You must do whatever is considered "reasonably practicable" to do this.

You must therefore make sure that workers and others (contractors, visitors, and the general public) are safe and protected from anything that may cause harm to them. So, you must look at and control risk of an injury or ill health that may arise in the workplace.

Below I have listed the basics of what is either required or generally considered best practice.

Health & Safety Policies

Your company must have a Health & Safety Policy in place if you employ 5 or more employees. Even if you don't have 5 employees, it is good practise to have a policy in place.

This helps in a couple of areas such as having a basic policy to work to but also so that you can show your prospective clients or even when having an audit carried out that you are acting in a positive manner.

How to write your policy

Your policy should cover three areas.

Part 1: Statement of intent

State your general policy on health and safety at work, including your commitment to managing health and safety and your aims. As the employer or most senior person in the company, you should sign it and review it regularly.

Part 2: Responsibilities for health and safety

List the names, positions, and roles of the people in your business who have specific responsibility for health and safety.

Part 3: Arrangements for health and safety

Give details of the practical arrangements you have in place, showing how you will achieve your health and safety policy aims. This could include, for example, doing a risk assessment, training employees, and using safety signs or equipment.

The law

The legal requirement to write a policy is included in the Health and Safety at Work etc Act. The Management of Health and Safety at Work Regulations explain the steps you must take to manage health and safety.

Risk Assessments

Whatever your business, your employees undertake tasks to fulfil their duties. To enable them to do this safely the employer should undertake a Risk Assessment of the tasks to ensure that employees are not placed in danger and either the hazard is eliminated or there is a control measure in place.

A basic risk assessment that every business will need nowadays is a DSE assessment (Display Screen Equipment). Essentially this is a workstation assessment and it looks at all sorts of things such as the equipment, furniture, and work conditions as well as the job being done and also any special requirements a member of staff may have.

The assessment should include information of who will perform the task, what the hazard might be, identify the risk, what additional equipment is required to reduce the risk (or eliminate it), or if there is an alternative option.

Other common risk assessments needed are manual handling, even in offices. Think about how heavy a couple of boxes of paper can be when they're dumped in reception by the delivery person and they need shifting to the 3rd floor office for instance.

You will also need to consider more complex risk assessments for the more complicated tasks that are required. Depending on your industry, you will need to consider different things, but here's a few for you to consider, some obvious and some not so obvious:

- Slips, trips, and falls
- Working at height
- Manual handling
- Working in confined spaces
- Working on electrics
- Working near electrics
- Working with machinery
- Working with hand tools
- Delivering goods
- Working in inclement weather
- Working near water
- Lone working

How to assess the risks in your workplace

- Identify the hazards
- Decide who might be harmed and how
- Evaluate the risks and decide on precautions
- Record your significant findings
- Review your assessment and update if necessary

Identify the hazards

One of the most important aspects of your risk assessment is accurately identifying the potential hazards in your workplace. A good starting point is to walk around your workplace and think about any hazards. In other words, what is it about the activities, processes or substances used that could injure your employees or harm their health?

When you work in a place every day it is easy to overlook some hazards, so here are some tips to help you identify the ones that matter:

- **Check manufacturers' instructions** or data sheets for chemicals and equipment as they can be very helpful in spelling out the hazards and putting them in their true perspective

- **Look back at your accident and ill-health records** - these often help to identify the less obvious hazards

- **Take account of non-routine operations** (e.g. maintenance, cleaning operations or changes in production cycles)

- **Remember to think about long-term hazards to health** (e.g. high levels of noise, exposure to harmful substances, common causes of work-related mental ill health)

- **Visit the** HSE website. HSE publishes practical guidance on hazards and how to control them

There are some hazards with a recognised risk of physical harm, for example working at height, working with chemicals, machinery, asbestos and also some with a risk of work-related mental ill-health e.g. where demands, control and support for individuals are not properly managed in the workplace. Depending on the type of work you do, there may be other hazards that are relevant to your business.

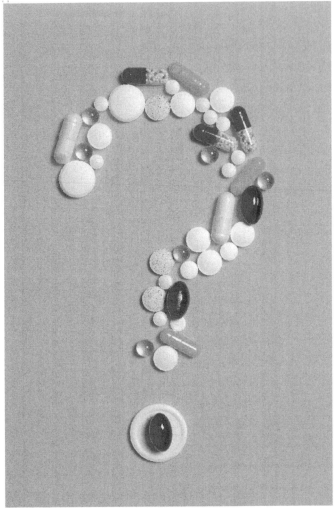

Decide who might be harmed and how

Think how employees (or others who may be present such as contractors or visitors) might be harmed. Ask your employees what they think the hazards are, as they may notice things that are not obvious to you and may have some good ideas on how to control the risks.

For each hazard you need to be clear about who might be harmed; it will help you identify the best way of controlling the risk. That doesn't mean listing everyone by name, but rather identifying groups of people (e.g. 'people working in the storeroom' or 'passers-by').

Remember:

- Some workers have particular requirements, for example new and young workers, migrant workers, new or expectant mothers, people with disabilities, temporary workers, contractors, homeworkers, and lone workers
- Think about people who might not be in the workplace all the time, such as visitors, contractors, and maintenance workers
- Take members of the public into account if they could be hurt by your activities
- If you share your workplace with another business, consider how your work affects others and how their work affects you and your workers. Talk to each other and make sure controls are in place
- Ask your workers if there is anyone you may have missed

Evaluate the risks

Having identified the hazards, you then have to decide how likely it is that harm will occur; i.e. the level of risk and what to do about it. Risk is a part of everyday life and you are not expected to eliminate all risks. What you must do is make sure you know about the main risks and the things you need to do to manage them responsibly.

Generally, you need to do everything 'reasonably practicable'. This means balancing the level of risk against the measures needed to control the real risk in terms of money, time, or trouble. However, you do not need to take action if it would be grossly disproportionate to the level of risk.

Your risk assessment should only include what you could reasonably be expected to know - **you are not expected to anticipate unforeseeable risks.**

Look at what you're already doing, and the control measures you already have in place. Ask yourself:

- Can I get rid of the hazard altogether?
- If not, how can I control the risks so that harm is unlikely?

Some practical steps you could take include:

- trying a less risky option
- preventing access to the hazards
- organising work to reduce exposure to the hazard
- issuing protective equipment
- providing welfare facilities such as first aid and washing facilities
- involving and consulting workers

Improving health and safety need not cost a lot. For instance, placing a mirror on a dangerous, blind corner to help prevent vehicle accidents is a low-cost precaution considering the risks. Failure to take simple precautions can cost you a lot more if an accident does happen.

Involve your workers, so that you can be sure that what you propose to do will work in practice and won't introduce any new hazards.

If you control a number of similar workplaces containing similar activities, you can produce a 'model' risk assessment reflecting the common hazards and risks associated with these activities.

You may also come across 'model' assessments developed by trade associations, employers' bodies or other organisations concerned with a particular activity. You may decide to apply these 'model' assessments at each workplace, but you can only do so if you:

- satisfy yourself that the 'model' assessment is appropriate to your type of work
- adapt the 'model' to the detail of your own work situations, including any extension necessary to cover hazards and risks not referred to in the 'model'

Record your significant findings

Make a record of your significant findings - the hazards, how people might be harmed by them and what you have in place to control the risks. Any record produced should be simple and focused on controls.

If you have fewer than five employees, you don't have to write anything down. It is useful to do this however so you can review it at a later date, for example if something changes. If you have five or more employees, you are required by law to write it down.

Any paperwork you produce should help you to communicate and manage the risks in your business. For most people this does not need to be a big exercise - just note down the main points about the significant risks and what you concluded.

When writing down your results keep it simple, for example 'Fumes from welding: local exhaust ventilation used and regularly checked'.
A risk assessment must be 'suitable and sufficient', i.e. it should show that:

- a proper check was made
- you asked who might be affected
- you dealt with all the obvious significant hazards, taking into account the number of people who could be involved
- the precautions are reasonable, and the remaining risk is low
- you involved your employees or their representatives in the process

Where the nature of your work changes fairly frequently or the workplace changes and develops (e.g. a construction site), or where your workers move from site to site, your risk assessment may have to concentrate more on a broad range of risks that can be anticipated.

Identify long-term solutions for the risks with the biggest consequences, as well as those risks most likely to cause accidents, and work-related physical or mental ill-health. You should also establish whether there are improvements that can be implemented quickly, even temporarily, until more reliable controls can be put in place.

Remember, the greater the risk the more robust and reliable the control measures will need to be.

Review your risk assessment and update if necessary

Few workplaces stay the same. Sooner or later, you will bring in new equipment, substances and procedures that could lead to new hazards. So, it makes sense to review what you are doing on an ongoing basis, look at your risk assessment again and ask yourself:

- Have there been any significant changes?
- Are there improvements you still need to make?
- Have your workers spotted a problem?
- Have you learnt anything from accidents, near misses, work-related ill-health (physical and mental) reports, sickness absence data or employee surveys?

Make sure your risk assessment stays up to date.

Another way to think about risk assessments is to use the acronym ERIC, this stands for:

Eliminate

If you can eliminate an identified hazard by taking a different decision, you must do this; (1) if it is a mandatory requirement or a specific obligation; but otherwise (2) so far as reasonably practicable.

Reduce

If the hazard cannot be eliminated, you must reduce the remaining risks associated with the hazard, so far as reasonably practicable. And then;

Inform

Provide information on risks to those that may be involved in the task and what the control measures will be.

Control

Providing the task, the working environment and no other influences come to bear, the control of the risks is the responsibility of those undertaking the work.

When reducing risks, there is a hierarchy to be observed, which is known as the 'general principles of prevention'.

COSHH Assessments

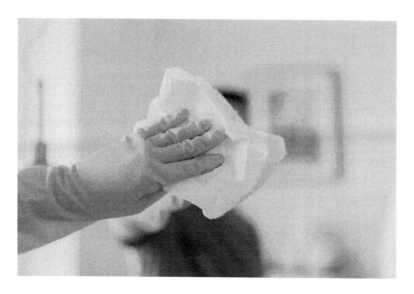

If products and materials are used, then it may be necessary for the employer to provide a COSHH Assessment (Control of Substances Hazardous to Health).

In smaller companies it could be as simple as cleaning products and how they are stored and used. Even something minor like changing the toner on a copier should have a COSHH assessment as this will also indicate disposal methods.

More complex assessments may include use and storage of chemicals either in liquid or powder form or even gases that are used.

Exactly what you need will depend on your industry, but here's a few for you to consider, some obvious and some not so obvious:

- Bleach
- Toilet cleaner

- Acids
- Petrol
- Diesel
- Butane
- Paints

How to assess the risks in your workplace

Before you start your COSHH assessment, you need to:

Think about

- What do you do that involves hazardous substances?

- How can these cause harm?

- How can you reduce the risk of harm occurring?

Always try to prevent exposure at source. For example:

- Can you avoid using a hazardous substance or use a safer process – preventing exposure, e.g. using water-based rather than solvent-based products, applying by brush rather than spraying?

- Can you substitute it for something safer – e.g. swap an irritant cleaning product for something milder, or use a vacuum cleaner rather than a brush?

- Can you use a safer form, e.g. can you use a solid rather than liquid to avoid splashes or a waxy solid instead of a dry powder to avoid dust?

Check your trade press and talk to employees. At trade meetings, ask others in your industry for ideas.

If you can't prevent exposure, you need to control it adequately by applying the principles of good control practice.

Control is adequate when the risk of harm is 'as low as is reasonably practicable'.

This means:

- All control measures are in good working order.

- Exposures are below the Workplace Exposure Limit, where one exists.

- Exposure to substances that cause cancer, asthma or genetic damage is reduced to as low a level as possible.

Most product suppliers provide a product data sheet which can be used as a basis for your COSHH assessment.

Procedure Manuals / Operating Procedures

Most employers have employees perform different tasks to each other and as such there should be a Procedures Manual for the different activities so everyone is aware of the activities and how they are performed.

Many may interact, and employees must be aware of how this is done. A procedures manual is also good to keep track of the tasks that are carried out in your organisation. This helps when training and inducting new staff members as it's all written down and removes the element of "from memory". Some tasks may not be carried out every single day and it's easy to forget a step when carrying out such an infrequent task whereas the procedures manual can be consulted and the person carrying out the task can refresh their memory instead of just cracking on.

General principles

There have been numerous recorded incidents where failings by operators have been the major contributing cause of major accidents. Provision of clear, concise, and accurate operating procedures is the most effective measure to prevent, control and mitigate such events.

Operating procedures should clearly lay down instructions for operation of process plant that take into consideration COSHH, manual handling, permit to work, PPE Regulations, quality, HAZOP, and SHE requirements. The procedure should represent a definition of good or best practice that should be adhered to at all times. Process operatives should be provided with guidance concerning the required operating philosophy to ensure that they comply with procedural requirements.

Adequate training should be provided to ensure that operators are fully conversant with written procedures.

It is important that operating procedures should always reflect plant practice, and vice versa.

Provision of Comprehensive Written Operating procedures

Comprehensive written operating procedures should be generated where applicable that address:

- Standard operating procedures and operating philosophy;
- Abnormal operating procedures;
- Temporary operating procedures;
- Plant trials;
- Emergency operating procedures;
- Commissioning;
- Plant Start-up;
- Plant Shut-down;

- Bulk loading and unloading;
- Process change;
- Plant change.

These procedures should cover the following:

- Material safety data (COSHH);
- Plant operatives should have an awareness and understanding of material safety data for raw materials, intermediates, products and effluent / waste;
- Control measures and personal protective equipment;
- Location of plant where process is to be undertaken;
- Roles and responsibilities of individuals involved in plant operations;
- Plant fit for purpose;
- The condition of main process plant and equipment (clean, empty etc. as appropriate) should be established as being fit for purpose;
- The condition of ancillary process plant and equipment (clean, empty etc. as appropriate);
- Plant correctly set up for processing;
- Process monitoring and recording;
- Monitoring and recording of key process parameters (temperature, pressure etc.) in plant logs;
- Quality;
- Sampling of raw materials, intermediates, products and effluent/waste;
- Packaging of final product.

Operating procedures should be controlled documents, generally covered under the company's quality system and thus kept fully up to date. Any changes should be fully controlled and documented and should be subject to company change procedures. Standard operating procedures may be revised for the following reasons:

- Introduction of new equipment into the process;
- Introduction of new chemicals into the process;

- Significant change to process, task, personnel or equipment covered by the procedure;
- Plant trials have been successful and need to be incorporated into standard operating procedures.

Limits of Intervention, Control Systems Interface

Clear demarcation of where limits of intervention cease and reliance upon the control systems interface begins is a critical step in defining the operating procedures for a given plant or process. During the hazard and operability stage, the justification of reliance upon human intervention rather than automated systems should be established. This should be assessed in more depth in a subsequent risk assessment.

Commissioning procedures

Commissioning of process plant is the practical test of the adequacy of prior preparations, including training of operating personnel and provision of adequate operating instructions. Since the possibility of unforeseen eventualities cannot be eliminated during this period when operating experience is being gained, the need for safety precautions should be reviewed. This should form part of the HAZOP / Risk Assessment processes applied to the installation. Full written operating instructions should be provided for all commissioning activities.

Commissioning Procedures document a logical progression of steps necessary to verify that installed plant is fully functional and fit for purpose. A general sequence of steps in commissioning may typically include:

- System Configuration Check;
  The purpose of this activity is to trace all pipework and connections to verify the system configuration, and to visually inspect items of equipment to ensure that they

are clean, empty and fit for purpose as appropriate prior to undertaking water trials.

- Instrumentation System Check - Verification of Alarms and Trips;
  The purpose of this activity is to ensure that all instrumentation, alarm settings, microprocessor signals and hardwire trips pertaining to the installation are functional. This will also check that signals from the field instrumentation are displayed locally and are being correctly relayed to the computer interface rack, as well as to the computer system.

- Flushing and Cleaning of Lines and Vessels with Water;
  The purpose of this activity is to clean all items of pipework and the vessels that make up the installation. This task shall also ensure that there are no obstructions, blockages, or any potential contaminants in any of the process lines or vessels that may have resulted from materials being left inside the system from the construction phase. If chemicals incompatible with water are to be used, it is important that the pipelines and equipment are thoroughly dried prior to introduction of the chemicals. This is normally done by passing dry air through the plant.

- Assessment of Ancillary Equipment;
  The main aim of this assessment is to verify the performance of all ancillary equipment. This may include pumps, fans, heat exchangers, condensers etc.

- Calibration of Vessels and Instrumentation;
  The purpose of this activity is to check the calibration and performance of all vessels and instrumentation pertaining to the installation. To a certain extent this will be carried out in conjunction with the system pre-checks to ensure that the correct set points and alarm points have been established for use in the water trials.

- Start Up Protocol;
  The purpose of this procedure is to provide guidance for bringing the installation online starting from an empty non-operational system.

- Shut Down Protocol;
  The purpose of this procedure is to provide guidance for taking the installation offline starting from a fully operational system.

- Chemical Trials;
  The aim of this activity is to verify the performance of the installation by simulating 'live' conditions by following standard procedures.

- Handover
  Each section should be read in detail to gain understanding about the particular requirements of the activity prior to undertaking the activity itself and completing the associated check list. The checklist will serve as a permanent record of the activity, and can be reviewed if future modifications are undertaken.

It is assumed that prior to the commencement of commissioning activities that full support from plant personnel has been obtained.

Start-up / shutdown procedures

Many potential hazards can be realised during start-up or shutdown of plant or process. Specific operating procedures should be provided which take account of all eventualities. For some specific plant items, start-up is known to present particular additional hazards; some examples of these are:

- Dryers – when starting up a drying system after maintenance or a plant shut-down, the actual temperature the dryer might reach before settling out with the control system may result in an increased chance of a dust explosion;

- Furnaces – explosions may occur if ignition of fuel is delayed;

- Vessels, Tanks, Reactors – ignition of flammable vapours introduced may occur for systems relying on elimination of oxygen to prevent explosions, unless inert gas purging is carried out effectively;

- Reactors – start-up of batch reactors after agitator failure may cause an uncontrollable exothermic reaction.

The start-up and shut-down procedures should be ordered and phased so that interlinked plant operations can resume or cease in a safe and controlled manner.

Emergency procedures

Any potential deviations to normal operation that cannot be addressed by design or control identified in the Hazard and Operability studies should be covered by emergency procedures. These should detail how to make plant and process safe, minimising risks to operators at all stages. They should cover PPE, the level of intervention which is safe and when to evacuate. The procedures will need to tie in closely with the on and off-site emergency plans provided under COMAH.

Management / supervision

A clear management structure should be in place that defines competent responsible person(s) for generation of operating procedures and supervision of plant and personnel. The role of the supervisor in terms of training of operators is overseeing certain critical operations and checking logs and other activities to ensure compliance with operating procedures. This should fulfil the requirements of the company's health and safety policy.

Human factors

The appropriate design of a procedure is critical in the reduction of human error within process operations. The benefits of procedures are that they can aid an operator when they are faced with a complex diagnosis, or they can act purely as an aide memoir during non-critical routine operations.

The following section provides human factors guidance on the production and implementation of procedures.

Generally, there are four types of procedure:

- Procedures that provide general operating guidance;
- Procedures that provide an aid to meeting operating aims;
- Procedures that are mandatory and prescribe behaviour; and
- Procedures that are used as a training tool.

Each of the procedure types listed above all conform to the same general human factor's principals. These are discussed below.

Task analysis
The content of important procedures should be based on some form of formal task analysis method to ensure that the procedure accurately describes the task it refers to. On some plants a process may have a safety-related action or task that has become an accepted 'unofficial' part of the procedure, but which is not documented anywhere. In this situation the task analysis will pick up on this and allow it to

be incorporated into the procedures. Conversely, any dangerous actions that an operator might routinely carry out will also be detected.

The most commonly used method of task analysis is Hierarchical Task Analysis (HTA). Further information on this method and others can be found in 'A Guide to Task Analysis' edited by B. Kirwan and L. K. Ainsworth.

Operating instructions should be close to the user and kept up to date. The following issues should be considered in assessing operating procedure documentation:

- There should be no easier, more dangerous alternatives than following the procedure.
- There should be a suitable QA system in place to ensure that the procedures can be kept up to date and that any errors are quickly detected and hence corrected.
- The procedures should not be needlessly prescriptive. The best way of ensuring that procedures do not become overly prescriptive is through involving the operator during the design stage.
- Procedures should contain information on the requirements for the wearing of personal protective equipment during the task.
- Any risks to the operator should be documented at the start of the procedure, based on a risk assessment of the task.
- An appropriate method of coding each procedure should be used.
- Each time a procedure is produced it should be dated and also marked, where appropriate, with a shelf life, i.e. 'This procedure is only valid for six months after the date hereon'.
- There should be no ambiguity between which procedures apply to which situations.
- Procedures do not always have to be paper based.

- At the start of the procedure an overview of the task should be provided.
- Prerequisites should be presented clearly at the start of the procedure to ensure that the operator can check that it is safe to proceed.
- The most important information on the page should be identified and this should be designed to be the most prominent information.
- Separate headings should be used to differentiate clearly between sub tasks.
- Any warnings, cautions or notes should be placed immediately prior to the instruction step to which they refer.
- Language should be kept as simple as possible, i.e. use nomenclature familiar to the operator.
- The nomenclature should be consistent with that on controls or panels.
- Symbols, colours, and shapes used for graphics should conform to industry standards.

Validation

A procedure should always be formally validated prior to it being issued. The best method to achieve this is a comprehensive walk-through assessment of the procedure in the plant, or with reference to the relevant plant drawing when an in-plant assessment is not possible.

Fire Risk Assessments

The place of work should have a Fire Risk Assessment, and this should be undertaken at least annually or if there is a change of building layout or activity that may introduce additional risk.

If available, building layout drawings should be viewed and compartmentation identified.

The fire risk assessment looks at means of escape and can highlight things needed such as signage, firefighting equipment, smoke / heat detectors, sprinkler systems, dry risers and alarm systems.

General fire safety hazards

Fires need three things to start – a source of ignition (heat), a source of fuel (something that burns) and oxygen:

- sources of ignition include heaters, lighting, naked flames, electrical equipment, smokers' materials (cigarettes, matches etc), and anything else that can get very hot or cause sparks

- sources of fuel include wood, paper, plastic, rubber or foam, loose packaging materials, waste rubbish and furniture
- sources of oxygen include the air around us

What do I have to do?

Employers (and/or building owners or occupiers) must carry out a fire safety risk assessment and keep it up to date. This shares the same approach as health and safety risk assessments and can be carried out either as part of an overall risk assessment or as a separate exercise.

Based on the findings of the assessment, employers need to ensure that adequate and appropriate fire safety measures are in place to minimise the risk of injury or loss of life in the event of a fire.

To help prevent fire in the workplace, your risk assessment should identify what could cause a fire to start, i.e. sources of ignition (heat or sparks) and substances that burn, and the people who may be at risk.

Once you have identified the risks, you can take appropriate action to control them. Consider whether you can avoid them altogether or, if this is not possible, how you can reduce the risks and manage them. Also consider how you will protect people if there is a fire.

- Carry out a fire safety risk assessment
- Keep sources of ignition and flammable substances apart
- Avoid accidental fires, e.g. make sure heaters cannot be knocked over
- Ensure good housekeeping at all times, e.g. avoid build-up of rubbish that could burn
- Consider how to detect fires and how to warn people quickly if they start, e.g. installing smoke alarms and fire alarms or bells

- Have the correct fire-fighting equipment for putting a fire out quickly
- Keep fire exits and escape routes clearly marked and unobstructed at all times
- Ensure your workers receive appropriate training on procedures they need to follow, including fire drills
- Review and update your risk assessment regularly

Fire Marshalls & Fire Wardens

Alongside the Fire Risk Assessment, as duty holder you should ensure that you have competent people to organise evacuation in an emergency.

These are called Fire Marshalls or Fire Wardens. They must be trained to understand the layout of the building, where refuge points are located, to guide staff to the assembly points and to check that all staff are accounted for.

There should be signing in/out procedure for all staff and visitors to enable this.

Training Fire Marshalls / Fire Wardens

Training for Fire Marshalls / Wardens should cover:

- UK Health and Safety Law – cover the basics

- The principles of fire risk assessment – requirements and how to complete an assessment
- Recording the findings – the legal requirements plus communication, monitoring and review
- Role of the Fire Warden – how to plan for an emergency, roll calls, sweeping the building and daily requirements

Asbestos

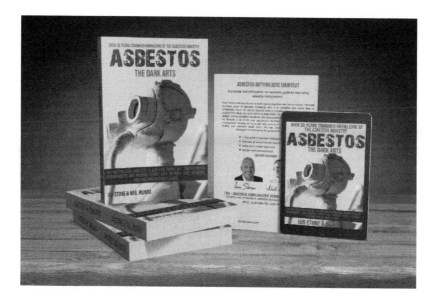

Asbestos was banned in the UK in November 1999. It is the biggest industrial killer in the UK. In 2020 it is killing over five thousand people per year in the UK alone.

In 2020 it is killing over five thousand people per year in the UK alone.

This is why to cover off asbestos the HSE have produced a whole set of regulations concerning asbestos. It is a complex area, so complex in fact that Ian Stone and Neil Munro the two directors of Acorn Safety wrote a book all about the subject and how to comply. The book was Asbestos The Dark Arts which is a number 1 bestseller.

OVER 30 YEARS COMBINED KNOWLEDGE OF THE ASBESTOS INDUSTRY

ASBESTOS

THE DARK ARTS

THE DUTYHOLDERS SHORTCUT TO ASBESTOS KNOWLEDGE, UNDERSTANDING REQUIREMENTS AND KEEPING PEOPLE SAFE WITHOUT OVER SPENDING, WASTING TIME OR GOING IT ALONE

IAN STONE & NEIL MUNRO

Here we provide a basic rundown of this complex set of regulations and detail everything you need in place.

The HSE has bountiful amounts of information within their website. However, some of it is not so easy to traverse and understand. As with the rest of this book, our aim is to provide you with the most information in the easiest to understand format.

7 Steps to Asbestos Management Heaven!

The following overview highlights what is required to be fully asbestos compliant with Regulation 4. We have summarised the regulation and what is required.

Step 1. Identify Asbestos
Step 2. Record Findings
Step 3. Assess the Risk
Step 4. Management Plan
Step 5. Make Asbestos Safe
Step 6. Communicating and Sharing
Step 7. Reviewing and Updating

Step 1. Identify Asbestos

Dutyholders are required to identify or presume asbestos materials are present within their property and check their condition.

The easiest way to identify if asbestos materials are present within a property is to have an asbestos survey. Asbestos surveys will be explained further in the next chapter. However, a management survey is generally used to provide this level of information. As the name suggests, asbestos management surveys provide the asbestos information required to manage asbestos on a day-to-day basis.

A management survey is the easiest route. However, there is the option of presuming asbestos materials. In reality, this is not very practical because we already know that asbestos was used in over 5,000 products – that's a lot of presumptions in a building!

With asbestos management, you have to:

PRESUME IT'S ASBESTOS UNTIL YOU CAN PROVE IT'S NOT!

Without evidence of whether materials are asbestos or not, you have to presume everything is. In reality, this is just not practical to operate on a day-to-day basis within your property and/or business.

Any material known or presumed to contain asbestos must be kept in a good state of repair. Therefore, the condition of the asbestos materials must be assessed. This assessment is called a material risk assessment.

This book advocates that the dutyholder can complete a lot of things themselves. However, some things we believe should be left to the experts.

It makes no sense for a layperson to take the risk of identifying asbestos-containing materials on their own. In UKAS, accredited companies' surveyors are only let loose once they are deemed competent to do so.
It is, however, the dutyholder's responsibility to ensure that the survey completed is to the correct standard.

Step 2. Record Findings

Dutyholders are required to ensure that a written record of the asbestos is made and that the record is **kept up to date**.

A written record, usually referred to as an asbestos register, and site plan detailing asbestos locations, presumed locations and areas not accessed should be completed.

Again, the easiest way to complete this is with a management survey! Or, you can get your pen and paper out and get writing, a lot! For your own assessment to be worth its weight, it will need to have been completed in line with *HSG264: Asbestos The Survey Guide.* As previously mentioned, guidance complies with ACoPs, Regulations and Acts, which we want to stay on the right side of.

Once the survey or written records (register and drawing plans) have been completed, they MUST be kept up to date. All too often, dutyholders have surveys completed but fail to do anything beyond this point.

The register and plans must be live documents all up to date and reflecting the current conditions. If the condition of the asbestos changes (material risk changes), if asbestos materials are removed and even if areas of the building change, these documents must be updated.

Step 3. Assess the Risk

Dutyholders are required to assess the risk of anyone being exposed to these asbestos materials.

Managing asbestos means preventing people from breathing in asbestos fibres. Assessing the likelihood of exposure to asbestos will help you to comply with your legal duties.

Priority Risk Assessments (PRAs) can help you determine the likely risk of people being exposed to asbestos from the materials present within your building. Or, in other words, help you identify the risk of the asbestos being disturbed by someone in your building and them being exposed to it.

These assessments also help you to set a priority as to what needs to be actioned first. The overall risk is determined from the risk of the material and the risk to the occupants.

This one should be a joint approach at least. You can save money and time by having the asbestos surveyor complete these for you. The cost increase to complete PRAs is usually negligible. However, the most important aspect of having these completed by the surveyor is to then go through them and check they are correct!

The surveyor can only use their best guess when completing these. Therefore, it is imperative that you check the data. After all, you know your building and you'll have a better knowledge of its occupants and activities within it.

If you want to save money or if you want to gauge a real understanding about PRAs, you can complete them either by following the steps in HSG264 or by using the PRA tool, which can be found here:

https://tinyurl.com/yceu8vdv

This form allows you to use the information from the survey to then generate your own PRAs. Or you can use this to check the PRAs that have been completed on your behalf by the surveying company.

Step 4. Asbestos Management Plan

Dutyholders are required to ensure that a written plan to manage the asbestos risk is prepared and that the plan is put into effect.

The asbestos management plan (AMP) should set out how the identified asbestos risks should be managed. The most important thing here is whatever you plan to do you must put into action.

Depending upon your site, this is going to be really easy or really difficult to put together.

Step 5. Make Asbestos Safe

Dutyholders are required to ensure that any material known or presumed to contain asbestos is managed accordingly. Factors such as the location, condition and frequency of access, will determine the action required e.g., repair, physical protection or removal.

Asbestos works may need to be completed following appropriate assessments. An appropriate contractor who is trained, insured and/or licensed to work with asbestos will be required.

Certain types of works will also require accredited independent asbestos air testing.

The main purpose for asbestos work isn't to remove asbestos unless it's necessary – it should be to ensure that it's safe and manageable.

Step 6. Communicating and Sharing

Dutyholders are required to ensure that information regarding the asbestos is provided to anyone who is liable to disturb it or who is potentially at risk.

Asbestos information must be provided by the dutyholder to anyone likely to come into contact with asbestos in their buildings.

This can be achieved in a number of ways, e.g. hard copies of surveys, electronic copies of surveys and online asbestos survey databases.

Again, depending upon the size and complexity of the estate, one or more ways may be required to ensure the information is shared accordingly.

Databases should no longer be expensive to buy or to utilise. We provide a FREE online database for all our clients – it's included in the price for whatever we complete.

There are database companies still charging exorbitant fees for setup and use per gigabyte storage. In the predominantly online world that we now live in, this simply shouldn't be charged for.

The only times that fees should be incurred are when the system is needed to do something out of the ordinary and the developer's time is needed.

For a standard online database, you should be paying **ZERO, £0.00, NOTHING**! We have clients with thousands upon thousands of sites held and their cost is **ZILCH**.

For an online database, you should be paying ZERO, £0.00, NOTHING! We have clients with thousands upon thousands of sites held and their cost is ZILCH.

Step 7. Reviews and Updates

As a minimum, the asbestos management plan, including records and drawings, should be reviewed and updated every 12 months.

Annual asbestos reinspections and annual management plan audits should be undertaken.

Again, this is something you may be able to do if you are competent. However, it would be our recommendation to utilise a surveying company for the same reasons as getting a survey undertaken.

It eliminates your risk and also saves time because all documents associated with the reinspection need to be updated, along with the Asbestos Register, AMP, the PRAs and also the online database.

First Aid

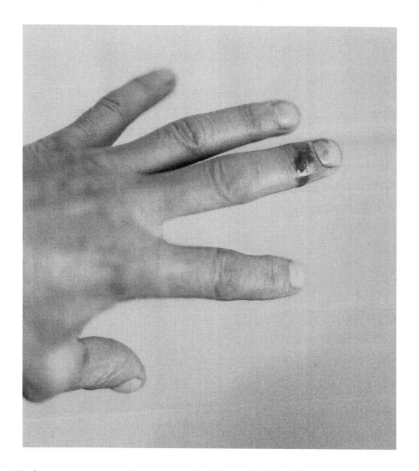

To keep your employees safe, First Aid facilities should be available.

You must have: a suitably stocked first aid kit and an appointed person or people to take charge of first aid arrangements. There must be information for all employees telling them about the first aid arrangements you have in place.

How to be First Aid Ready

As a minimum, a low-risk workplace such as a small office should have a first-aid box and a person appointed to take charge of first-aid arrangements, such as calling the emergency services if necessary. Employers must provide information about first-aid arrangements to their employees.

Workplaces where there are more significant health and safety risks are more likely to need a trained first aider. A first-aid needs assessment will help employers decide what first aid arrangements are appropriate for their workplace.

What should a first-aid box in the workplace contain?

The decision on what to provide will be influenced by the findings of the first-aid needs assessment. As a guide, where work activities involve low hazards, a minimum stock of first-aid items might be:

- a leaflet giving general guidance on first aid (for example, HSE's leaflet Basic advice on first aid at work);
- individually wrapped sterile plasters (assorted sizes), appropriate to the type of work (hypoallergenic plasters can be provided if necessary);
- sterile eye pads;
- individually wrapped triangular bandages, preferably sterile;
- safety pins;
- large sterile individually wrapped unmedicated wound dressings;
- medium-sized sterile individually wrapped unmedicated wound dressings;
- disposable gloves (for advice on latex gloves please see Selecting latex gloves)

Many people are not aware that first aid items have an expiry date, just like many other things. Make sure you check the dates on the items, so they remain in date for use.

Appointed Persons

What is an appointed person?

When an employer's first-aid needs assessment indicates that a first aider is unnecessary, the minimum requirement is to appoint a person to take charge of first-aid arrangements. The roles of this appointed person include looking after the first-aid equipment and facilities and calling the emergency services when required. They can also provide emergency cover, within their role and competence, where a first aider is absent due to unforeseen circumstances (annual leave does not count).

Do appointed persons need to undertake first-aid training?

To fulfil their role, appointed persons do not need first-aid training. However, emergency first-aid training courses are available.

How many first aiders do I need?

The findings of your first-aid needs assessment will help you decide how many first aiders are required. There are no hard and fast rules on exact numbers, and you will need to take into account all the relevant circumstances of your particular workplace.

Suggested numbers of first-aid personnel to be available at all times people are at work:

From your risk assessment, what degree of hazard is associated with your work activities?	How many employees do you have?	What first-aid personnel do you need?
Low-hazard, e.g. offices, shops, libraries	Fewer than 25	At least one appointed person
	25–50	At least one first aider trained in EFAW
	More than 50	At least one first-aider trained in FAW for every 100 employed (or part thereof)
Higher-hazard, e.g. light engineering and assembly work, food processing, warehousing, extensive work with dangerous machinery or sharp instruments, construction, chemical manufacture	Fewer than 5	At least one appointed person
	5–50	At least one first aider trained in EFAW or FAW depending on the type of injuries that might occur
	More than 50	At least one first aider trained in FAW for every 50 employed (or part thereof)

Health and Safety Law Posters

If you employ anyone, you must either display the Health and Safety Law poster where your workers can easily read it or provide each worker with the equivalent health and safety law leaflet.

The poster explains British health and safety laws and lists what workers and their employers should do.

ACORN SAFETY

The Health and Safety Information for Employees Regulations 1989 requires employers to either display the HSE-approved law poster or to provide each of their workers with the equivalent leaflet.

You should add details of any employee safety representatives or health and safety contacts to the poster or leaflet.

Consulting Employees

You must consult all your employees on health and safety.

You can do this by listening and talking to them about health and safety and the work they do, how risks are controlled, the best ways of providing information and training.

Consultation is a two-way process, allowing employees to raise concerns and influence decisions on managing health and safety. Your employees are often the best people to understand risks in the workplace. Involving them in making decisions shows that you take their health and safety seriously. In a small business, you might choose to consult your workers directly. Larger businesses may consult through a health and safety representative, chosen by your employees or selected by a trade union. As an employer, you cannot decide who the representative will be.

What does the law say?

The law sets out how you must consult your employees in different situations and the different choices you have to make. There are two sets of general regulations about your duty to consult your workforce about health and safety:

- The Safety Representatives and Safety Committees Regulations 1977

- The Health and Safety (Consultation with Employees) Regulations 1996

These regulations will apply to most workplaces.

These regulations are designed to enable you and your employees to work together:

- to develop, maintain and promote measures that ensure health and safety at work; and

- to check the effectiveness of such measures.

You may only have to consult under one set of regulations, or you may have to consult under both, depending on circumstances.

The presence of a union health and safety representative does not prevent managers from communicating directly with the workforce as a whole. Managers remain responsible for managing health and safety in the workplace and should consult the workforce as necessary.

Existing arrangements

Where you already have existing consultation arrangements that satisfy health and safety law, you do not have to change them. However, you may want to review your arrangements to make sure that they are the right ones for your organisation now.

Disagreements

If you and your employees disagree about the interpretation of these regulations, you should first use your usual procedure for resolving employment relations disputes. You may find it helpful to involve the Arbitration and Conciliation Service (Acas). However, health and safety inspectors (from HSE and local authorities) can enforce for failure to comply with legal duties on procedural matters. They will decide what action to take in line with HSE's Enforcement Policy Statement.

Training Needs

Everyone who works for you needs to know how to work safely and without risk to their health. This includes contractors and self-employed people.

You must give your workers clear instructions and information, as well as adequate training. Make sure you include employees with particular training needs, for example new recruits, people changing jobs or taking on extra responsibilities, young employees and health and safety representatives.

Keeping training records will help you decide if refresher training is needed. Health and safety training should take place during working hours and must be free for employees. Staff will need extra training if you get new equipment or your working practices change.

For health and safety representatives to be able to perform their functions, they need to be equipped with appropriate skills and knowledge, so you must plan for their training.

Training for health and safety representatives appointed by trade unions

If you have health and safety representatives appointed by trade unions, the trade union will arrange to train them.

Trade unions offer online training courses, so health and safety representatives may not always have to leave the workplace, but may simply require access to online training within the workplace and time to complete the course.

Training for elected health and safety representatives

If your workforce has elected health and safety representatives, you must ensure they are provided with time off with pay to undergo training for their role.

Identify training needs

It is helpful for all new health and safety representatives to have training that will cover:

- the role of the representative, including how to communicate in committee meetings, with colleagues for views, with employers to raise issues, and with health and safety inspectors;
- health and safety legislation;
- how to identify and minimise hazards and dangerous occurrences;
- health and safety issues of new technology; and
- how to carry out a workplace inspection and accident investigation (not required but recommended for non-union elected representatives)

Welfare Facilities

Employers must provide Welfare Facilities (see table below) and a working environment that is healthy and safe for everyone in the workplace, including those with disabilities.

You must have:

- the right number of toilets and washbasins
- drinking water and somewhere to rest and eat meals
- a healthy working environment – a clean workplace with a reasonable working temperature, good ventilation, suitable lighting and the right amount of space and seating
- a safe workplace – well-maintained equipment, with no obstructions in floors and traffic routes, and windows that can be easily opened and cleaned

Temporary worksites

You must provide flushing toilets and running water, for example with a portable toilet. If this is not possible, use alternatives such as chemical toilets and water containers.

The following tables show the minimum number of toilets and washbasins that you should provide.

Number of toilets and washbasins for mixed use (or women only)

Number of people at work	Number of toilets	Number of washbasins
1-5	1	1
6-25	2	2
26-50	3	3
51-75	4	4
76-100	5	5

Toilets used by men only

Number of people at work	Number of toilets	Number of urinals
1-15	1	1
16-30	2	1
31-45	2	2
46-60	3	2
61-75	3	3
76-90	4	3
91-100	4	4

Reporting Under RIDDOR

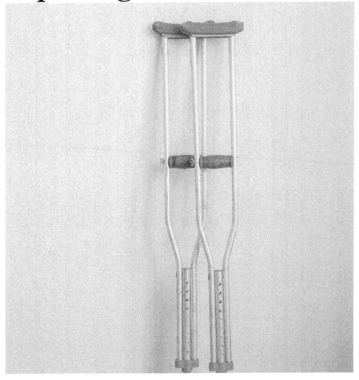

Under law, you must report certain workplace injuries, near-misses and cases of work-related disease to HSE. This duty is under the Reporting of Injuries, Diseases and Dangerous Occurrences Regulations, known as RIDDOR.

RIDDOR puts duties on employers, the self-employed and people in control of work premises (the Responsible Person) to report certain serious workplace accidents, occupational diseases and specified dangerous occurrences (near misses).

Who should report?

Only 'responsible persons' including employers, the self-employed and people in control of work premises should submit reports under RIDDOR.

Reporting online

Responsible persons should complete the appropriate online report form listed below. The form will then be submitted directly to the RIDDOR database. You will then have the option to download a copy for your records.

- Report of an injury
- Report of a dangerous occurrence
- Report of a case of disease
- Report of flammable gas incident
- Report of a dangerous gas fitting

Telephone

All incidents can be reported online but a telephone service is also provided for reporting fatal/specified incidents **only** - call the Incident Contact Centre on 0345 300 9923 (opening hours Monday to Friday 8.30 am to 5 pm).

Keeping Records

If you have more than 10 employees, you must keep an accident book. You can buy one from HSE Books or similar or record the details in your own record system.

Keeping records of incidents helps you to identify patterns of accidents and injuries, so you can better assess and manage risk in your workplace.

Records can also be helpful when you are dealing with your insurance company. Make sure you protect people's personal details by storing records confidentially in a secure place.

A health record must be kept for **all** employees under health surveillance.

Records are important because they allow links to be made between exposure and any health effects. Health records, or a copy, should be kept in a suitable form for at least 40 years from the date of last entry because often there is a long period between exposure and onset of ill health.

What information should be included in health records?

Individual, up-to-date health records must be kept for each employee placed under health surveillance. These should include details about the employee and the health surveillance procedures relating to them.

Employee details should include:

- surname
- forename(s)
- gender
- date of birth
- permanent address, including post code
- National Insurance number
- date present employment started

Recorded details of each health surveillance check should include:

- the date they were carried out and by whom
- the outcome of the test/check
- the decision made by the occupational health professional in terms of fitness for task and any restrictions required. This should be factual and only relate to the employee's functional ability and fitness for specific work, with any advised restrictions.

The record should be kept in a format that can be linked with other information (e.g., with any workplace exposure measurements).

If you are collecting an historical record of jobs or tasks completed during current employment involving exposure to identified substances requiring health surveillance, it is useful to store them with this record.

For some exposures, all you need to do is set up and maintain records that may be viewed alongside other information, such as air sampling or biological monitoring results. This is the case, e.g., with work involving:

- known or suspected carcinogens - **except** those listed in The Control of Substances Hazardous to Health (Fifth edition)
- machine-made mineral fibres (MMMF)
- rubber manufacturing and processing, giving rise to rubber process dust and rubber fume - except health surveillance/medical surveillance needed for India rubber manufacturing in COSHH
- leather dust in boot and shoe manufacture

It is good practice to offer individual employees a copy of their health record when they leave your employment. If your company changes hands, consider offering the health record to the individual employee, and/or to the new occupational health service provider. Make sure that health records are stored securely.

What health records should not contain

Health records are different to medical records in that they should not contain confidential medical information. Health records and medical records must therefore be kept separate to avoid any breaches of medical confidentiality.

Any personal medical information should be kept in confidence and held by the occupational health professional responsible for the health surveillance programme.

Medical records

Medical records are compiled by a doctor or nurse and may contain information obtained from the individual during the course of health surveillance. This information may include clinical notes, biological results and other information related to health issues not associated with work. This information is confidential and should not be disclosed without the consent of the individual.

The occupational health (OH) professional may obtain data as the result of an immunisation programme (for example, blood titres or 'non responder' information). This information will be provided to the employee and should not be given to the employer. It will be kept in confidence by the OH professional and should only be made known to the employer with the employee's consent.

The doctor or nurse should only provide employers with information on fitness to work and any restrictions that may apply in that respect. Employees can have access to their own medical record through a written request under the Data Protection Act. These details can only be released to third parties, such as the employer, on receipt of the informed written consent of the employee, or by a court order.

Competent Person & Retained Consultants

The Management of Health and Safety Regulations say that each company must appoint a Competent Person or people to help you meet your health and safety legal duties.

This can be a person from within the company but as an employer, you must ensure that any individual performing a task on your behalf has the competence to do so without putting the health and safety of themselves or others at significant risk.

If your business or organisation doesn't have the competence to manage health and safety in-house, for example, if it's large, complex or high risk, you can get help from a consultant or adviser. But remember, as the employer, managing health and safety will still be your legal duty.

Sadly, 97% of businesses will never reach full health and safety compliance. It's not their fault, they just haven't got the time or knowledge to do it all themselves.

A good health and safety consultant should be able to offer you a fully inclusive package to ensure you are compliant, rather than offering you everything as a piecemeal service which will cost a lot more.

Below is the kind of thing you should be looking for and also the benefits they bring to ensure you're fully protected:

Initial health and safety audit and review so you can find out exactly where you are with your health and safety compliance and identify what needs to be done.

"Competent Person" Certificate for you to display at your premises as proof that you have appointed a professional and competent Health & Safety Consultant in your business.

Win more business by designating your "Competent Person" for health and safety on company literature, tender documents and prequalification questionnaires e.g. SSiP Forum Members such as CHAS, Safe Contractor, Construction Line, etc.

Stay ahead of the competition with an annual consultation meeting with a health and safety consultant to discuss your on-going requirements and identify new work equipment, work procedures etc.

Keep up to date with regular updates on Health & Safety legislative changes and industry best practice procedures, saving you time, money and hassle.

Prepare a bespoke Health and Safety policy document including; policy statements, roles, responsibilities and arrangements written by an experienced and qualified health and safety professional removing the risk from you of getting it wrong.

Asbestos Compliance Audit in accordance with the Control of Asbestos Regulations 2012. Helping you identify if you are compliant and highlighting any gaps.

UNLIMITED advice when you really need it with a direct number and email facility for Health & Safety advice

Prepare your general Risk Assessments for company activities so you don't have to.

Prepare your COSHH assessments so you know it's done properly.

Assist with pre-qualification and tendering questionnaires helping you answer those tedious and difficult health & safety questions, not only saving you time but also reducing your stress.

Flexible company internal visits to support you with meeting your health and safety duties on behalf of the company. e.g. inspections, audits, reports etc.

Asbestos Starter Pack All the tools you'll need to get you managing your asbestos. Books, CDs, guides, infographics.

Undertake Fire Risk Assessment of your company premises so you know you, your team members and buildings are fire safe.

Produce an Asbestos Management Plan to enable you to meet your requirements under the Regulation 4 of The Control of Asbestos Regulations 2012.

CHAPTER 7

Additional Resources

Additional information about health and safety

The following is a list of additional resource websites that can be visited for further reading and information.

There are all sorts here from the Health and Safety Executive to other government bodies, trade associations and independently run websites.

Acorn Health and Safety
www.acornhealthandsafety.co.uk
A multi-disciplined health & safety consultancy. Whatever health and safety service you're looking for, whether it is undertaking a fire risk assessment, carrying out CDM consultancy services or completing site safety inspections and audits, we have the expertise and certifications to complete any health and safety requirement.

HSE (Health and Safety Executive)
www.hse.gov.uk
The HSE's work covers a varied range of activities; from shaping and reviewing regulations, to producing research and statistics and enforcing the law.

Environment Agency

https://www.gov.uk/government/organisations/environment-agency/services-information

The Environment Agency is a non-departmental public body, established in 1995 and sponsored by the United Kingdom government's Department for Environment, Food and Rural Affairs, with responsibilities relating to the protection and enhancement of the environment in England.

UKATA (UK Asbestos Training Association)

www.ukata.org.uk/asbestos-awareness

UKATA sets standards in asbestos training and ensures that its members meet those standards. Any organisation that allows builders or maintenance personnel onto their premises should ensure that they have evidence of asbestos awareness training. UKATA provides a quality standard for that training. When asbestos is to be worked upon deliberately, using a UKATA member to provide that training ensures that the training provider has the facilities, knowledge and experience to properly undertake that training.

UKAS (United Kingdom Accreditation Service)

www.ukas.com

The United Kingdom Accreditation Service is the sole national accreditation body recognised by government to assess, against internationally agreed standards, organisations that provide certification, testing, inspection and calibration services. Accreditation by UKAS demonstrates the competence, impartiality and performance capability of these evaluators. All companies that have obtained UKAS accreditation can be found listed on this site.

Constructionline

www.constructionline.co.uk

Constructionline platform to identify construction suppliers, membership is a must. Buyers use our platform to quickly find suppliers that will enable them to complete a whole range of projects. We validate all of our members, providing those buyers with a pool of high quality suppliers that they can confidently engage with.

SMAS Worksafe

www.smasltd.com

SMAS Worksafe is the leading SSIP scheme of choice, allowing thousands of contractors to quickly and simply demonstrate their commitments to workplace safety. Since the launch of SSIP, many construction companies and Principal Contractors now adopt this approach to Health & Safety pre-qualification and will only use contractors who hold a valid and in-date scheme certificate issued by an SSIP Member Scheme.

A key aim of the SSIP Forum is to reduce the burden and cost of H&S bureaucracy across the construction industry and as part of this, your SMAS H&S certificate will be recognised by other SSIP members who offer mutual recognition.

CHAS

www.chas.co.uk

CHAS, The Contractors' Health and Safety Assessment Scheme, is the Foremost Authority on UK compliance, Risk Mitigation and Supply Chain Management. We Will Help You to Gain Accreditation, Safeguard Your Reputation and Grow Your Business.

Alcumus SafeContractor

www.safecontractor.com

SafeContractor delivers a tailored health and safety accreditation allowing contractors to showcase their capabilities to potential customers.

Ian Stone

I've written a little bit about myself, so you can get to know who's behind the book. I'm married to my wonderful wife Sian and together we have an amazing little boy called Jaxon. He's the funniest kid that either of us know – he's forever making his own jokes up and making us laugh. He's a veracious reader, and I'm really proud of him and his achievements so far.

I love all things motorcycle, especially the IOM TT and the Moto GP – what those riders do is amazing. I love to cook outside on barbecues or in wood-fired ovens and really enjoy socialising with friends and family especially in the summer.

The downside to all the fun bits that most people enjoy is that I'm an asbestos geek. I started in the asbestos industry in 2002 and have carried out all manner of jobs in the industry.

It's an affliction, as once you're in the asbestos industry it's rare that you leave, but I love it! I really enjoy assisting people to move from a place of headache to asbestos freedom.

I hold the Certificate of Competence in Asbestos and am a Fellow member of the Royal Society for Public Health. I also hold several proficiency module qualifications in asbestos and occupational hygiene. With these qualifications, you can be safe in the knowledge that the advice you receive is that of a proven expert.

My asbestos career has been slightly more eclectic than most, which has helped provide such an overview of the asbestos industry and issues surrounding asbestos management.

I am a qualified and competent surveyor, air analyst, bulk analyst and consultant who has worked within both UKAS and Non UKAS organisations.

As well as working on the asbestos consultancy side of the industry, I have also worked on the asbestos removal contracting side by helping a business obtain their 1-year and then 3-year asbestos removal licence.

For over three years, I left day-to-day practice to become the Manager of ATaC, the leading asbestos trade association for Asbestos Testing and Consulting businesses in the UK. During my time, I helped develop new asbestos industry qualifications through the RSPH (Royal Society for Public Health).

Whilst at ATaC, I also lobbied Parliament, working with the Asbestos in Schools steering group, which was at the time headed up by Michael Lees MBE. Michael was honoured by the Queen for the amazing work he had completed following the death of his wife 13 years previous from mesothelioma.

After working together for a number of years, I approached several MPs to write letters of support along with an application for Michael to be honoured. Michael was subsequently honoured with an MBE on the Queen's birthday honours list as a Campaigner and Founder of Asbestos in Schools Group for services to the Wellbeing of Children and Teachers.

I re-joined practice after ATaC and I am now a Director of Acorn Analytical Services and Acorn Safety Services, which are asbestos and health and safety consultancies respectively. I assist with the running of the business as well as providing impartial and practical consultancy advice to businesses.

ABOUT THE AUTHORS

Neil Munro

I'm Neil. I thought you might like to find out a little bit about me. As of 2020 I'm 40 years old – wow, it's strange seeing that in writing, as in my head I still feel like I'm 19, although the grey hairs say something different. I'm lucky to be married to my best mate, Eleanor. We celebrated 10 years of marriage on 11th October 2018.

Together, we have been very fortunate to have two children, our son Reid and our daughter Freya.

It's great having one of each – one minute, I can be playing *Minecraft* and the next, I'm putting clothes on one of the hundreds of dolls who seem to be taking over our home.

I love eating! Whether it's eating out, take-aways, BBQs or cooking at home, I love a good meal. Whenever I look at the menu, my first thoughts are always *what's the biggest thing on here?*

Now, I know this is probably painting a bad picture of me, but, in fact, all the above is more of a treat and I take everything in moderation.

In fact, I have the most disciplined diet of anyone I know, much to the humour of my work mates. I like to keep myself fit, which does allow for some of those extra treats now and again.

I've been in the asbestos industry since 2003 and I can't get away from it. If I'm not working around asbestos, I'm reading articles about it, writing articles about it, training people about it... I've even got pictures of it on the walls in my house.

This passion of mine has given me the knowledge and experience to help clients whatever the asbestos situation may be.

I'm a fully qualified and competent asbestos surveyor, air monitoring analyst, bulk analyst, consultant and trainer. I have worked within a number of UKAS accredited, Non UKAS accredited and asbestos removal contractor organisations. This has given me invaluable experience within all areas of the asbestos industry.

I am a Fellow member of the RSPH and hold a multitude of proficiency certificates in asbestos inspection, testing and licensed asbestos removal management. I've been an asbestos trainer for many years.

During my time working for an asbestos removal contractor, I was actively involved and instrumental in the company achieving two major milestones. Firstly, was successfully gaining UKAS accreditation as an inspection body and secondly, was being granted a full HSE license to work with asbestos. As a new company, all quality manuals, risk assessments, controlled documents, procedural documents had to be produced, rolled out, verified and audited accordingly.

As the founding Director of Acorn Analytical Services Northampton office and Acorn Health and Safety, I've had the pleasure of helping a vast range of clients complete their projects, always on time, always within budget.

I work with clients to not only ensure that they become compliant, but more importantly that they understand what they need to do.

Glossary of Terms
A list of the abbreviations and acronyms often used

AALA (Adventure Activities Licensing Authority)
AALR (Adventure Activities Licensing Regulations)
ACOPs (Approved Codes of Practice)
ACSNI (Advisory Committee on Safety in Nuclear Installations)
AFARP (As far as reasonably practicable)
AGGM (Advisory Committee on Genetic Manipulation)
ALARP (As low as reasonably practicable)
AMP (asbestos management plan)
AOR (artificial optical radiation)
ATaC (Asbestos Testing and Consultancy)
ATP (Automatic Train Protection)
BASEEFA (British Approvals Service for Electrical Equipment In Flammable Atmospheres)
CAR (Control of Asbestos)
CAWR (Control of Asbestos at Work)
CBI (Confederation of British Industry)
CDG (Carriage of Dangerous Goods)
CDM (Construction Design Management)
CHAS (Contractors' Health and Safety Assessment)
CIMAH (Control of Industrial Major Accident Hazard Regulations)
COMAH (Control of Major Accident Hazards Regulations)
COSHH (Control of Substances Hazardous to Health)
DEFRA (Department for Environment, Food and Rural Affairs)
DSE (display screen equipment)
EA (Environment Agency)
EHO (Environmental Health Officer)
EU (European Union)
FFI (Fee for Intervention)
FRA (Fire Risk Assessment)
H&S (Health and Safety)
HASWA (Health and Safety at Work Act)
HAZOP (hazard and operability study)

ACORN SAFETY

Glossary continued:

HSC (Health and Safety Commission)
HSE (Health and Safety Executive)
HSL (Health and Safety Laboratory)
HTA Hierarchical Task Analysis
LA (Local Authority)
LPG (liquefied petroleum gas)
NADOR (Notification of Accidents and Dangerous Occurrences Regulations)
ND (Nuclear Directorate)
NII (Nuclear Installations Inspectorate)
NSC (Nuclear Statutory Corporation)
NSRM (Nuclear Safety Research Management Unit)
OCNS (Office for Nuclear Security)
ONR (Office for Nuclear Regulation)
ORR (Office of Rail and Road)
OSCR (Occupational Safety Consultants Register)
OSHCR (Occupational Safety Consultants Register)
POW (Plan of Work)
PPE (Personal Protective Equipment)
PRAs (Priority Risk Assessments)
PSD (Pesticides Safety Directorate)
PUWER (Provision and Use of Work Equipment Regulations)
RA (Risk Assessment)
RAMS (Risk Assessment Method Statement)
REACH (Registration, Evaluation, Authorisation and Restriction of Chemicals)
Regs (Regulations)
RLSD (Research and Laboratory Services Division)
ROSPA (Royal Society for the Prevention of Accidents)
RPE (Respiratory Protective Equipment)
RSPH (Royal Society for Public Health)
SACGM(CU) Scientific Advisory Committee on Genetic Modification (Contained Use)
SFAIRP (so far as is reasonably practicable)
SHE (Safety, Health & Environment)
SMEs (small and medium-sized enterprises)
SMRE (Safety in Mines Research Establishment)
TUC (Trades Union Congress)
UK (United Kingdom)
UKAEA (United Kingdom Atomic Energy Authority)
UKAS (United Kingdom Accreditation Service)
UKATA (United Kingdom Asbestos Training Association)
UKSO (UK Safeguards Office)

Are You Still Looking to Remove Your Health and Safety Headache?

Do you want help instead of going it alone?

Claim Your Complimentary <u>Audit</u>* Worth

£597.00

Are you sure you're legally compliant?

Go here now and claim:

<u>www.acornhealthandsafety.co.uk/contact-us</u>
In the "How Can we Help You" Box type "Book Audit"

For a limited time, we're offering you a 20-minute strategy session where we'll discuss your business goals and challenges and draw up a H&S Blueprint for you for free.

*Please note this is NOT a sales call. You will be speaking with one of our highly experienced Consultants, not a salesperson.

Printed in Poland
by Amazon Fulfillment
Poland Sp. z o.o., Wrocław